SHE
VOTES

SHE VOTES

★★★★★★★★★★★★★★★

HOW U.S. WOMEN WON SUFFRAGE, AND WHAT HAPPENED NEXT

BY BRIDGET QUINN   FOREWORD BY NELL IRVIN PAINTER

✦✦✦✦✦✦✦✦✦✦✦✦✦

WITH ILLUSTRATIONS BY 100 WOMEN ARTISTS

CHRONICLE BOOKS
SAN FRANCISCO

Text copyright © 2020 by Bridget Quinn.
Foreword copyright © 2020 by Nell Irvin Painter.
Images copyright © 2020 by Chronicle Books LLC.

Library of Congress Cataloging-in-Publication Data

Names: Quinn, Bridget, author. | Painter, Nell Irvin, author of foreword.
Title: She votes : how U.S. women won suffrage, and what happened next / by
  Bridget Quinn ; with a foreword by Nell Painter ; with illustrations by
  100 women artists.
Identifiers: LCCN 2019047183 | ISBN 9781452173160 (hardcover)
Subjects: LCSH: Women—Suffrage—United States—History—Juvenile
  literature. | Suffragists—United States—Juvenile literature.
Classification: LCC JK1898 .Q56 2020 | DDC 324.6/230973—dc23
LC record available at https://lccn.loc.gov/2019047183

Manufactured in China.

Design by Allison Weiner.
Typesetting by Frank Brayton.
Images coordinated by Mallory Farrugia.
Jacket illustrations by Libby VanderPloeg (front), Dani Pendergast
(back left), and Simone Martin Newberry (back right).

10 9 8 7 6 5 4 3 2

Chronicle Books LLC
680 Second Street
San Francisco, California 94107
www.chroniclebooks.com

FOR ZUZU
REBEL GIRL & QUEEN OF MY WORLD

BUT WE'LL HAVE OUR RIGHTS; SEE IF WE DON'T: AND YOU CAN'T STOP US FROM THEM; SEE IF YOU CAN.
—SOJOURNER TRUTH

PROCEEDINGS OF THE WOMAN'S RIGHTS CONVENTION
HELD AT THE BROADWAY TABERNACLE, IN THE CITY OF NEW YORK,
ON TUESDAY AND WEDNESDAY, SEPT. 6TH AND 7TH, 1853.

SHE DID NOT MIND WORKING. SHE WORKED TO CULTIVATE HER VOICE.
—GERTRUDE STEIN

MISS FURR AND MISS SKEENE, 1922

CONTENTS

FOREWORD

★ ★ ★ ★ ★ ★ ★ ★ ★ ★ ★ ★ ★

BY NELL IRVIN PAINTER

HERE WE ARE, a century after the passage of the Nineteenth Amendment to the United States Constitution allowing women the vote— allowing women, a majority of the American citizenry, a say in their country's governance. This, truly, is an anniversary worthy of gigantic celebration. And celebration there is in this book, a work of fresh, deep understanding of women's suffrage as the foundation of women's rights.

Such a book has never been seen before, and I mean that literally. Here we have not only a bounty of witty words, historians' usual tools. Here also are images chosen with Bridget Quinn's especial skill as an art historian: one hundred artworks by one hundred women artists. An art bounty of women's empowerment.

Breadth of vision is *She Votes*'s enduring characteristic as an *intersectional* work. Quinn sees American women broadly, not simply the educated white women at the fore a century ago, and does not skip over the continued disfranchisement nor the agency of women of color. Quinn starts her definition of women's rights with the ability to hold and dispose of property, as embodied in Haudenosaunee women in upstate New York. Well before the event ordinarily recognized as the origin of women's rights, the Seneca Falls women's rights convention of 1848, Native women had what settler American women lacked: agency, property, and power. At Seneca Falls and throughout the nineteenth and twentieth centuries, non-Indian women struggled to gain their full rights as citizens.

Nell Irvin Painter, *Princeton Self-portrait*, 2015.

Inclusion is one of *She Votes*'s great strengths, as Quinn navigates a history of both expanded rights and the narrow-minded exclusion that emerged when suffrage expanded after the Civil War. The beloved antebellum community of feminist-abolitionists broke apart after the Civil War amendments enfranchised black men and inserted "male" into the United States Constitution. Ever since 1867, Americans have been arguing over whether woman suffragists and woman's suffrage were fundamentally exclusionary.

For some commentators, obviously racist comments by Elizabeth Cady Stanton, Susan B. Anthony, and early twentieth-century suffragists characterize the movement as a whole. For others, suffragism's comfortable fit into American white supremacy needs to be seen as a regrettable but not a defining part of the history of women's rights. Disagreements of this character persist, as in July and August 2018 columns in the *New York Times*. Threading between opposing views, Quinn never loses sight of the limitations, even the villainies, of woman suffrage within the prejudices prevailing in American society over time. In words and images, Quinn never narrows her own vision of American women.

Within its narrative of rewarding imagination, *She Votes* investigates and demolishes convenient founding myths: Was Susan B. Anthony actually in Seneca Falls in 1848? Evidently not. And did Sojourner Truth really ask whether or not she was a woman? Emphatically not. Thanks, Bridget Quinn, for a commemoration of the struggles for American women's rights, conceived and written broad-mindedly.

INTRODUCTION

THIS IS A TRUE STORY.

AN ADVENTURE STORY.

IT'S GOT TRIUMPHS, oh yes, but also its share of tragedy. Beautiful friendships and terrible betrayals. Greek myth–level hubris alongside earnest human striving and good will. It's a tale of hope and courage and, maybe most of all, the relentless pursuit of freedom. Liberation by way of persistence.

This is the remarkable and too-little-known story of how the Nineteenth Amendment to the United States Constitution, which prohibits states and the federal government from denying voting rights on the basis of sex, came to be adopted at last on August 18, 1920.

And what happened next.

★ ★ ★

IT'S NOT THE WHOLE STORY, not by a long shot. That would take more space than I've got here and maybe more time than you've got just now. Because the story is still being written every day, thank goodness, maybe by you.

So, here's what I propose on this particular docket: nineteen ways of looking at the history of women's rights in America.

Art has always been enlisted to memorialize the past, our fierce battles and grand achievements, our grievous losses and deepest sorrows. So, in commemoration of one hundred years since ratification of the Nineteenth Amendment, herein one hundred women artists illuminate our past and celebrate the badassery of our present.

"To create one's own world takes courage," said Georgia O'Keeffe. That goes for art and for politics. That goes for everything worthwhile, as we'll soon see.

Should I confess right up front that I'm more art historian than, ahem, capital "H" Historian? I'm more than willing to arm-wrestle over how much it matters. What I am mostly is a storyteller. And what I believe more than anything is that the stories of history need to be told. True stories, to quote Norwegian painter Edvard Munch, about "living people, who breathe, feel, suffer, and love."

Speaking of Norway, in 1913 it became the so-called "first sovereign nation" to grant women the right to vote. In Norwegian, the verb "to vote" is *stemme*, which is also the noun *voice*.

In any language, the right to vote means having a voice, using it, and making it heard.

With that in mind, I'm always interested in giving voice to women's lives, telling a history (dare I say herstory?) that's been overlooked and forgotten. Because there's a kind of murder of the spirit that happens when we forget where we've been and who made us, when we lose track of the gifts of our inheritance. Which are, like the boons of a fairy tale, the very tools to help us fashion our way forward.

★ ★ ★

HOW U.S. WOMEN GOT THE VOTE is a foundational story of American womanhood, a tale always worth telling anew. The story usually begins with the Seneca Falls Convention in 1848.

But let's not start there.

Let's start instead in a smallish bathroom in Arlington, Virginia, belonging to my old grad school pal Mark and his wife, Caren.

It was January 21, 2017, the morning after the inauguration of America's forty-fifth president, and I was brushing my teeth.

Seventy-five mornings earlier I'd been hunched over my computer at home in San Francisco, watching the 2016 presidential election unfold. I watched commentators across political parties, across websites, and across the country ratchet up the unease as presidential reality dawned. When the anxiety of following returns became too much (chest tight, mouth dry, anything in the house that didn't require cooking quickly consumed), I distracted myself with Facebook and Twitter. There, I repeatedly saw images of women leaving stickers on the grave of Susan B. Anthony, in the fittingly named Mount Hope Cemetery in Rochester, New York, until her modest gray headstone was brightly lacquered in round white stickers stamped with red script: I Voted Today! I Voted Today! I Voted Today!

Mount Hope.

The living redeeming the dead.

Or, as it turned out, attempting to. One hundred and eleven years after the death of Susan B. Anthony—imperfect icon of women's suffrage, who never (legally) voted and who did not live to see the Nineteenth Amendment passed—American women cast their votes for a major-party woman candidate for president for the very first time.

But Hillary Clinton did not win. Instead, a TV personality of recent "grab them by the pussy" notoriety became the forty-fifth man to win the presidency of the United States. It was a brutal one-two punch.

So a march was called for, and I'm guessing you know the rest, though you might not know that it wasn't the first time women organized a

protest march to coincide with a presidential inauguration. The Woman Suffrage Procession of 1913 was held the day before newly elected Democrat Woodrow Wilson was sworn into office for his first term.

More than eight thousand women marched that day, "in a spirit of protest against the present political organization of society, from which women are excluded," according to the day's official program. In other words, women demanded the vote.

The front of that same program depicts a trumpeting young white woman on a white horse at the head of the procession, her hair styled in a sleek bob in Joan of Arc meets "New Woman" flapper fashion. There really was a white woman on a white horse: one Inez Milholland, who would, like Joan of Arc herself, give up her life for the cause. There was so much courage involved in the fight for women's right to vote. There was also racism. When black suffragists were told to march in the back that day, journalist Ida B. Wells called bullshit. She marched with her home state of Illinois, then returned to Chicago, where she'd founded the Alpha Suffrage Club for black women seeking both gender and racial equality, and where she kept on working for both.

★ ★ ★

IN THE ARLINGTON BATHROOM, toothbrush in hand, I hoped that this once we might have learned from history. All evidence was to the contrary, though, because otherwise why would we need this Women's March on Washington at all? We had the vote and yet women's rights were still very much in peril.

My mind was racing over it all—where we'd been and where we'd ended up and how we got there and what was next—readying myself literally and metaphorically, when I noticed something behind me in the mirror.

There on the wall beside the shower curtain was a framed reproduction of Jacques-Louis David's *The Death of Marat*. This famous painting of the French Revolution depicts an instigator of the Reign of Terror bleeding out in his bathtub (Christ of the Jacobins).

The French bathtub in the painting and the American bathtub at my heel nearly touched, past and present, histrionic art history and quotidian square footage of tile in continuing conversation. To quote Barack Obama, who was paraphrasing William Faulkner: "The past isn't dead and buried. In fact, it isn't even past." I'd seen *The Death of Marat* in reproduction hundreds of times, but now I saw it with new eyes.

Marat was a radical journalist and ardent supporter of Maximilien Robespierre, architect of the Reign of Terror, which saw thousands executed by guillotine and other means. Before Marat's friends came to power, he sometimes hid from the authorities in the sewers of Paris, wherein he contracted an icky skin condition made bearable only by hot baths. So Marat conducted business from his bathtub, writing poisonous articles and receiving visitors there (yes, really). One of these was a young woman from Normandy named Charlotte Corday who, upon arriving in the capital, had bought a five-inch kitchen knife from a street vendor, then hidden it in her skirts. If the Paris big shots couldn't stand up to terror, she'd do it herself, by murdering Marat in his bath.

Looking at *The Death of Marat*, for once I didn't think about painter Jacques-Louis David, master of his craft (also a bit of a dick, but that's history for you), or the dying Jean-Paul Marat. Instead, for the very first time, I considered Charlotte Corday. Brave, idealistic, doomed Corday was the reason the painting existed. And she was nowhere in the picture.

I suddenly got Corday, her anger and her need to act (which is not to say I condone murder—I don't). Finished with my ablutions, I took a last glance at Marat, pulled on my pussy hat, and looked in the mirror. A blondish middle-aged woman in glasses and a black puffy jacket, the pockets stuffed with snacks for a long day outdoors, stared back. I smiled, showing some teeth. No Charlotte Corday for sure, but I would have to do.

★ ★ ★

STEPPING ONTO THE NATIONAL MALL

with my friends was like entering a living history painting: sprawling, heroic, timeless. Caren and I gaped at each other, mouths open in response to half a million high-spirited human beings gathering to protest. Mark had already been taking pictures on the crowded subway, but now he never lowered his camera.

"Courbet!" he said, laughing. I turned and, yes, there was Realist artist Gustave Courbet's pornographic 1866 painting *L'Origine du monde* (*The Origin of the World*), reproduced in perfect detail on a young woman's sign. I assure you that, more than a hundred and fifty years later, this exaltation of female anatomy had lost none of its shock value.

The woman held her sign higher and spun it around. It had white thighs on one side and black on the other, with VIVA LA PUSSY! written in big red sparkly letters above and below both pairs of spread legs. "We're art historians," Mark said, explaining our perhaps over-interest in her sign. "I am, too," she said, and we high-fived.

Art was everywhere. And I don't just mean the "codified" artworks reproduced on many signs (in addition to the Courbet, there was more than one version of Artemisia Gentileschi's *Judith Severing the Head of Holofernes*), but the whole performative parade. At the other end of 2017, the Women's March made many of the art world's year-end lists, including that of the *New York Times*. In *New York* magazine, critic Jerry Saltz listed "The Signs, Posters, and Clothing at the Women's March" as number one on his "10 Best Art Achievements of 2017."

A woman wearing glasses and a hijab walked by carrying a sign. It had an oval cut-out surrounded by a painted head covering, so that anyone sticking their head through would wear a hijab too. Big gold letters above the hole read: REGISTER ME! Like so much of the day, it was both funny and terrifying.

Women balanced in tree branches along the route, and shouted down to tell everyone what was happening, since by then we were pretty much immobilized by sheer numbers. From far away we could hear amplified voices, but no real words. Later I'd listen to the speakers online—from Angela Davis to Gloria Steinem, from America Ferrera to Kamala Harris—but at the time I just listened to the women in the trees.

A sign nearby said MONTANA WOMEN, written above five upraised fists of varying skin tones. As a proud native Montanan, I took out my phone to take a picture, just as a woman in a tree raised hers to do the same. The resulting image reminded me of Mary Cassatt's *In the Loge*, but instead of a man staring at a woman through his opera glasses while she looks elsewhere, we were two women who had each other in our sights. *I see you.* The idea cheered me.

Beyond the trees, a sliver of the Washington Monument was visible, which meant the Capitol building was somewhere up ahead. There, my cousin Terry Mimnaugh's statue of Jeannette Rankin stood in Emancipation Hall alongside busts of fellow suffragists Sojourner Truth and Susan B. Anthony. Rankin was the first woman elected to national office, four years before women got the right to vote. Her statue was one of Montana's contributions to the Capitol Rotunda, where each state gets to honor two of its most important citizens. I note here, with some fatigue, that out of one hundred state statues, just nine are of women.

There's also a sculpture dedicated to women's suffrage in the Rotunda: the *Portrait Monument*. At 14,000 pounds, it's a mini-Mount Rushmore. It depicts suffrage pioneers Lucretia Mott, Elizabeth Cady Stanton, and Susan B. Anthony, along with a ghostly fourth headstone of uncarved marble that legend says is meant for the bust of the first woman president. Though it was unveiled in the Capitol in 1921, the *Portrait Monument* has only been in the domed Rotunda since 1997,

when a bipartisan group of congresswomen insisted it come into the light. For more than three quarters of a century it had been stored underground in the Capitol Crypt, its inspiring original inscription forcibly removed by an official act of Congress. It had once read, in gold: "Men, their rights and nothing more. Women, their rights and nothing less." And: "Woman, first denied a soul, then called mindless, now arisen, declaring herself an entity to be reckoned."

WOMEN NOW ARISEN.

Standing between friends on the National Mall, surrounded by hundreds of thousands of women and men, reveling in signs and shouting, I was grateful for all the lives that brought us there. And cautiously hopeful.

And I thought of this quote, from Laguna Pueblo poet, academic, and activist Paula Gunn Allen: "The root of oppression is the loss of memory."

Moving forward, we should also look back.

CHAPTER 1

SENECA

I desire you would Remember the Ladies, and be more generous and favourable to them than your ancestors. Do not put such unlimited power in the hands of the Husbands. Remember all Men would be tyrants if they could. If perticuliar care and attention is not paid to the Laidies we are determined to foment a Rebelion.

**ABIGAIL ADAMS TO JOHN ADAMS
SECOND CONTINENTAL CONGRESS, PHILADELPHIA. 1776**

WHERE ARE THE WOMEN?

HAUDENOSAUNEE (IROQUOIS) ADVISERS TO BENJAMIN FRANKLIN, CONSTITUTIONAL CONVENTION, PHILADELPHIA, 1787

HISTORY LOVES A BIRTHDATE. So why not March 31, 1776, as the very one to mark the beginning of women's rights in America? That was when Abigail Adams wrote a letter to husband John (founding father and second president of the United States), saying, in essence: By the way, in the new code of laws that it will be necessary for you to make, maybe give women the same democracy you guys give yourselves; otherwise, we women "will not hold ourselves bound by any laws in which we have no voice or representation." Frankly, she could not have been more clear.

But—surprise!—women's rights found no place in the new constitution. Instead, seventy-two years passed between Abigail Adams's private letter and the public demands of the 1848 Seneca Falls Convention. It would be seventy-two years more before the Nineteenth Amendment granted women the political possibility of helping themselves. Seneca Falls was, quite precisely, the turning point.

If you know anything about the origin of women's rights in America, you've probably heard about Seneca Falls. Those two words may be pretty much all you know. Seneca Falls is one of those history word-packages like "Magna Carta" or "Teapot Dome Scandal" that has a familiar ring but . . . what was that about again?

For sure I did not learn about the Seneca Falls Convention in high school. I don't remember when I first "knew" about it. But here's what I thought I knew: In the mid-nineteenth century, some grim-faced and be-bunned white ladies held a meeting in upstate New York and got women the right to vote. The end.

But turns out the truth is more complicated, and far more interesting.

For one thing, why was such a momentous event held in a small, not-very-noteworthy upstate town? Why not New York City? Why not Washington or Boston or Philadelphia? As a writerly aside, if it was to be upstate New York then, dammit, why not Waterloo, just three miles west of Seneca Falls? Waterloo has such a wonderful ring. Then we'd call it: *Waterloo of the Patriarchy*. Nice.

Instead those three miles prevail and we have the Seneca Falls Convention. But the fact is, there's plenty of meaning to find there, too.

Because neither 1776 nor 1848 can be our true start date.

★ ★ ★

PICTURE SOMETHING LIKE THIS,

twenty-some years earlier: In the late 1820s, a Haudenosaunee woman tended squash, maize, and beans under a hot sun near her home. Her family (husband, children, mother, father, her sisters, their husbands, and children) were mostly all nearby. Like all Haudenosaunee families, hers was matrilineal, organized around women, who made things (food, clothing, art, etc.) and decisions (votes, for example) to secure the health and prosperity of their tribes. It had been that way for centuries, maybe forever.

That day, the woman had two visitors. First, a white playmate for one of her girls. Not unusual. Second, a man, now striding across the field, past the playing children, toward the main house. The kids parted for him. The woman stood and adjusted her loose tunic across her leggings, knocking dirt off her hands as she went out to meet the man.

He was interested in horses. She'd been expecting him. She nodded and they turned toward the barn, where she'd put a nice pair in stalls. It was dark inside, like night compared to the bright outdoors, and it took time for their eyes to adjust. When they reappeared at last, blinking in the bright sunlight, the woman was still on foot, but the man rode off on horseback.

As she walked toward her home, adjusting a leather pouch at her waist, she looked up to see her daughter's friend staring, mouth wide as a brainless fish.

She paused before the girl, concerned. This one had it hard—losing brothers one by one, and there were whispers that her father didn't care for daughters.

"What happened?" the girl whispered. She looked toward the barn. "With that man."

The woman opened the pouch at her waist, pointing to the money inside. "I sold him a horse," she said. The girl continued to look strange. It occurred to the woman that her daughter's friend might be a little dim-witted.

The girl pulled anxiously at her pigtails. "But what will your husband say?"

The woman bent down and looked into the girl's pale eyes: "It was my horse, so I can keep it or sell it. I do what I want with it."

Young Elizabeth Cady, future suffragist, never forgot it.

★ ★ ★

THE 1820S WERE PRETTY MUCH the pits for American girls, Natives excluded (though for Natives those years were certainly the pits for reasons other than gender inequality). The founding fathers, in their inimitable wisdom, had not in fact taken particular (nor *perticuliar*) care regarding *the Laidies* (despite Abigail Adams's persuasion). Instead they handled the rights of women in their new nation the same way they handled the unsettling problem of slavery: They kicked that shit down the road.

Somewhat ironic considering they'd borrowed the unifying ideals of the so-called Iroquois Confederacy (minus the matrilineal structures) to conjure a United States in the first place. By the way, Iroquois—a name of unknown etymology—is what European settlers called the Haudenosaunee, not what they call themselves.

It's an underknown fact that the "revolutionary" concept of a democratic union of discrete states did not spring fully formed from the Enlightenment pens of the founding fathers, like sage Athena from the head of Zeus. No, the idea of "united states" sprang from the Haudenosaunee, collective name for six tribes that comprise the so-called (mostly by non-Natives) Iroquois Confederacy: the Seneca, Oneida, Mohawk, Onondaga, Cayuga, and Tuscarora nations. Should you doubt this, check out Congressional Resolution 331, adopted in 1988 by the 100th Congress of the United States, which says as much. It's worth noting that the Haudenosaunee Confederacy still thrives today, likely the world's oldest participatory democracy.

What a shame, then, that in addition to a model of an indivisible democratic union, the founding fathers didn't also see in Haudenosaunee culture a new (to Europeans) and better model of gender parity.

But, nah.

Instead the laws of the new nation regarding women could hardly have been worse. Most of America's new legal system came from English common law (so much for rebellion). This meant, for example, that a married woman had zero rights as an individual. To wit: "By marriage, the husband and wife are one person in law: that is, the very being or legal existence of the woman is suspended during the marriage."

As the grown-up Elizabeth Cady Stanton would write in the Declaration of Rights and Sentiments: "He had made her, if married, in the eye of the law, civilly dead." A married woman in nineteenth-century America (and later) had no autonomy over her own body. There was no rape inside of marriage and beating your wife—within "reason"—was totally within the letter of the law. Wives being so often in need of moral correction and being quite shockingly willful and so on.

Furthermore, a married woman had no claim to personal possessions or money, including anything she brought into the

marriage or any money she might somehow earn. She also had no claims of custody for her children in the unlikely case of divorce. In fact, her children could be taken from her by her husband at any time—for any reason, or for no reason at all. She could not sign a contract, sit on a jury, bring a lawsuit, or leave her possessions to anyone but her husband at the time of her actual, physical death.

You might think single women had it better, and they sort of did. Unmarried women were at least autonomous human beings in the eyes of the law. But how to stay single? Not only did family, religion, and society all pressure women to marry, but there was the thorny problem of survival if you didn't. Education was mostly off limits, and professions where you could make an adequate wage certainly were. In the few occupations open to (single) women, they were paid far less than their male counterparts (by which I mean an even greater disparity than today).

The "choices" were nuts, to put it mildly. Choosing marriage meant giving up the self, plus giving birth to an average of seven children, with all the toil and heartache that entailed (childhood mortality was commonplace). Most married women were pregnant or nursing for between twenty to twenty-five years of their adulthoods. Many died in childbirth. Many others died young, their health worn out.

Unmarried women, meanwhile, were dependent on their parents or brothers or married sisters. So: no money, no sex, no real independence. Single women were likely to end up as nursemaids to sick relations and elderly parents, and/or de facto nannies

raising their siblings' children. Their social status could not have been lower.

All of the above was worse for poor women, who—married or unmarried—needed work, could hardly get it, and when they did were not fairly paid. And this may be obvious, but things were hardest for black women, even free black women.

One area where married and unmarried American women of all economic strata and races had parity was in voting. They couldn't. Because women themselves had no voice. Only men could write new laws that might allow women to come out from under their control. You see the problem.

★ ★ ★

BUT I DIGRESS. I'd started with geography and why Seneca Falls, though a small town even by nineteenth-century standards, was the ideal location for independent-minded women to make their stand.

For the Seneca and all the tribes of the Haudenosaunee Confederacy, power resided with the people. *All* the people. To clarify something from the introduction, Norway—though admittedly awesome—may have been the first sovereign nation to "give" women the right to vote, but Haudenosaunee women always had it.

Think of that little girl who was Elizabeth Cady, raised in upstate New York among the Haudenosaunee. She knew from much personal experience that there was such a thing on earth as women with rights.

The story of a white woman seeing a Native woman sell a horse appears in a few nineteenth-century accounts. In March 1888, ethnologist Alice Fletcher told a crowd at the first International Council of Women that she once saw a woman give away a horse. And according to Fletcher, when the woman was asked if her husband would be angry, her "eyes danced" and "breaking into a peal of laughter, she hastened to tell the story to the others gathered in her tent, and I became the target of many merry eyes. Laughter and contempt met my explanation of the white man's hold upon his wife's property."

If this sounds suspiciously like urban legend (rural legend?), here's Emma Borglum, wife of sculptor Solon Borglum (whose brother Gutzon carved Mount Rushmore), writing on her 1891 honeymoon in South Dakota: "One day I showed some astonishment at seeing a young Indian woman, in the absence of her husband, give two horses to a friend. She looked at me very coldly and said, 'These horses are mine.' I excused myself saying that in my country a woman would consult her husband before giving such expensive presents. The woman answered proudly, 'I would not be a white woman!'"

American women from New York to the Dakotas had eyes to see. And they saw that Native women had what they did not: agency, property, power.

★ ★ ★

SO SENECA WOMEN LIKELY INSPIRED

a handful of white women to take up the mantle of women's rights at Seneca Falls. But first those white ladies embraced abolitionism.

The 1840 World Anti-Slavery Convention was held in London. Some eight or so American women journeyed across the pond—with a large contingent of men—to represent the American Anti-Slavery Society abroad.

On hearing of the women's plan to participate, the British were appalled—even after it was pointed out that, hello, the British Empire from Canada to India to Australia was ruled by someone named Queen Victoria. Unmoved, British organizers pointed out that the Queen was not in attendance for a reason. She'd sent her husband, Prince Albert, to voice her deeply held anti-slavery views. Like the Queen herself, American women could quite properly have men speak for them.

Newlywed Elizabeth Cady Stanton was there with her husband, abolitionist journalist Henry Stanton. The fact that attending an anti-slavery convention overseas was their honeymoon tells you what kind of young people they were. In addition to not completely erasing her maiden name after getting hitched, Cady Stanton plucked an arrow from the Quakers' quiver by omitting the onerous phrase "obey" from her wedding vows. "I obstinately refused to obey one with whom I supposed I was entering into an equal relation," she later wrote. Since her formative childhood among the Haudenosaunee, she'd become a headstrong, forthright young woman, one understandably excited to join an international anti-slavery crusade. In London she expected radical company energized for change but was instead met with disgust. Given the opportunity to raise up women for an important fight, American clergy who'd disembarked before her had instead spent their first days in London "busily engaged in fanning the English prejudice into active hostility against the admission of these women into the Convention." After much eloquent debate, 90 percent of the worldwide delegates voted against women's participation in the convention.

But! So-called chivalry prevailed. In recognition of the fact that these determined American women had indeed sailed across the Atlantic, a somewhat perilous voyage filled with discomfort, time, and expense, in support of a noble cause, representing half the world's population—in *consideration* of all this, the delegates of the World Anti-Slavery Convention would allow women to be seated in a small space off the main hall behind a curtain so that they might listen in.

You're welcome, ladies! Deep bow, flourishing hand gesture, followed by patting self on back. . . .

★ ★ ★

THIS WAS THE FUEL twenty-five-year-old Cady Stanton would carry with her to Seneca Falls: "Burning indignation filled my soul."

In this way, striving to end slavery illuminated another oppression.

Disgusted, Cady Stanton turned to the most renowned American woman at the convention, Lucretia Mott, twenty years her senior, for guidance. Years later she recalled Mott as "the greatest wonder of the world—a woman who thought and had opinions of her own." Mott was both a prominent abolitionist and a celebrated orator. A description

that fit almost no other woman of the day. Women speaking in public was as unseemly as prostitution—simply not done by the right kind—and crowds sometimes tried to stop women from talking. Mott herself was often a target, and a mob once even threatened to burn her home. It's worth saying that no part of this was unique to America. As British classicist Mary Beard writes, "When it comes to silencing women, Western culture has had thousands of years of practice."

Crucially, Mott was a Quaker—another essential piece of the women's rights puzzle. The Quakers were sort of religious anarchists, throwing bombs into the hallowed mores of American society. In addition to not asking brides to "obey," Quakers welcomed women educators, even women preachers. Mott was herself a minister, which came in handy when clergy held up scripture as proof of God's male chauvinism. Master of theological jiujitsu, Mott handily dismantled such arguments.

She was also as committed as they come. Like many Quakers, she and her husband, James, were part of the Free Produce Movement, which meant they wouldn't use anything abetted by slave labor, meaning no sugar and no cotton, among other things. I'd say rum, but they were temperance activists, too. You know that line in *The Wild Ones* when someone asks Marlon Brando's character what he's rebelling against and he answers, "What've you got?" Lucretia Mott was like that. She'd take on anything. Or, almost.

Mott's ministry and her speeches against slavery to mixed audiences of Quakers and non-, men and women, made her one of the most famous and admired women of her

time. When the former slave and world-class orator Frederick Douglass first heard Mott speak, he said, "I saw before me no more a woman, but a glorified presence, bearing a message of light and love." And "whenever and wherever I have listened to her, my heart has always been made better and my spirit raised by her words."

In London, seasoned tactician Lucretia Mott and youthful warrior Elizabeth Cady Stanton found each other. Together they plotted revolution. Literally. According to Cady Stanton's *History of Woman Suffrage*, she and Mott didn't waste much time lollygagging behind a curtain, but "walked . . . arm in arm afterwards" and "resolved to hold a convention as soon as we returned home." That is, a convention for the rights of women.

It would take eight years.

★ ★ ★

PLENTY HAPPENED IN BETWEEN. For one thing, Cady Stanton had the first three of her seven children. And Mott was on constant tour, campaigning against slavery. Then the Stantons moved from lively Boston to sleepy Seneca Falls in 1847, a shift that Cady Stanton found dispiriting. So when, in the summer of 1848, her old acquaintance Lucretia Mott came to town—fresh off a month living among the Seneca people nearby—Cady Stanton jumped at an invitation to join her for tea. The party of five included herself; Mott; Mott's younger sister, Martha Coffin Wright, six months pregnant with her seventh child; and Mary Ann M'Clintock, mother of four daughters; at the home of Jane C. Hunt in—wait for it—the nearby town of Waterloo.

Yes, Waterloo at last. Napoleon himself would have quaked in the face of what Jane Hunt orchestrated. She invited four women (one of them famous) over to her house for afternoon tea on July 9, 1848, *two weeks after giving birth to her second child*. These were not women to be trifled with. Also the homes of both Hunt and M'Clintock were likely safe houses on the Underground Railroad. It was a heady gathering of activist mothers.

This afternoon tea—a tea party we might say, with all the attendant echoes of rebellion—was the powder keg for the war to come. All the women but Cady Stanton were Quakers, and if they weren't also temperance advocates we might wonder what those ladies had been drinking, because by the end of tea they'd committed to holding "a convention to discuss the social, civil, and religious condition and rights of woman." The first in American history, or maybe anywhere. In ten days' time.

Why so fast? Because they needed to do it while Lucretia Mott was still in town. She was their headliner and star. She was the bait in a brilliant bait and switch. People would come to hear Mott, then be offered the opportunity to endorse revolution.

That revolution came in the form of the Declaration of Rights and Sentiments, begun a few days later in Mary Ann M'Clintock's parlor around a smallish mahogany tea table, but mostly finished by Cady Stanton. The women struck on the idea of using the Declaration of Independence as their model, an exemplar of clarity and logic, and a document of self-evident importance in U.S. history. Some passages hewed close to the source, though even small tweaks were momentous. "We hold these truths to be self-evident: that all men and women are created equal." In other places, they went for the jugular: "The history of mankind is a history of repeated injuries and usurpation on the part of man toward woman, having in direct object the establishment of an absolute tyranny over her." Though radical for sure, such opinions were, let's say, expected. From there, though, things take a shocking turn.

"To prove this, let facts be submitted to a candid world." Of the seventeen "Sentiments" that followed, the first four speak to political rights, including two specifically referencing the vote:

He has not ever permitted her to exercise her inalienable right to the elective franchise; He has compelled her to submit to laws, in the formation of which she had no voice; He has withheld her from rights which are given to the most ignorant and degraded men—both natives and foreigners; Having deprived her of this first right as a citizen, the elective franchise, thereby leaving her without representation in the halls of legislation, he has oppressed her on all sides.

Cady Stanton took the Declaration home to edit the grievances, the first four of which

are above, and also the resolutions, the ninth of which was this: "Resolved, That it is the duty of women of this country to secure to themselves their sacred right to the elective franchise."

The passages on voting rights were Cady Stanton's alone, and they discomfited even her activist friends and family.

Henry Stanton, her husband, assisted in devising many of the document's legal arguments, but felt that demanding the vote for women went too far. "You will turn the proceedings into a farce," he said, before leaving town so as to disavow any connection with so doomed a cause. Daniel Cady, her father, got wind of things and hopped a train headed directly her way, so he could confirm that his daughter had not in fact gone insane.

Even brilliant, brave Lucretia Mott, willing to take on slaveholders, sugar plantations, and the liquor lobby, was aghast. "Why Lizzie, thee will make us ridiculous."

★ ★ ★

BUT GUESS WHAT? Lizzie did it anyway.

CHAPTER 2

VOICES CARRY:

SOJOURNER TRUTH

Although knowledge may not triumph over myth, it becomes at least a rival.

NELL IRVIN PAINTER
SOJOURNER TRUTH: A LIFE, A SYMBOL.

ON WEDNESDAY, MAY 28, 1851, at ten A.M., Akron's Universalist Old Stone Church (the "finest stone church in Ohio") was packed to overflowing. Hundreds of men and women filled the pews and aisles, crowding the front door and spilling into the street. Even the well-known lady editor of the Pittsburgh *Saturday Visiter*, late but insistently pushing forward, found sitting space only by crouching on the pulpit steps.

Old Stone Church was nicely situated on Akron's High Street overlooking the cool blue ribbon of the Little Cuyahoga River, but inside the air was likely stifling. Too many people, too much excitement; a great deal of physical and emotional heat. Less than three years after Seneca Falls, Akron was already hosting the second Ohio Woman's Rights Convention. Hundreds had answered the call sounded by local journal the *Anti-Slavery Bugle* for another convention. Among them was a former slave, abolitionist, suffragist, mother, and lauded preacher named Sojourner Truth.

Truth was one of several women (and men) who spoke that day (an "army of talent," raved the *Bugle*), but she was the only black woman to ascend the pulpit and speak out for women's equality. When she strode to the front of the church, tall and wiry, notable for her erect carriage and confident bearing, her mostly white audience came to attention. "May I say a few words?" she said. Taller than most women, Sojourner Truth seemed to rise a little higher. She leaned in and so did her audience. "I want to say a few words about this matter," she said, with disarming understatement. *This matter.* If only Truth were more widely remembered today for her subtlety, and humor.

If you're familiar with anything about Sojourner Truth, there's a good chance it's her solemn visage. You've probably seen her face on T-shirts, buttons, and postage stamps. With a gaze that feels like she's staring straight into your soul. Maybe you've seen Truth, as I did recently, looking out from a set of coasters at the National Civil Rights Museum in Memphis, alongside a set bearing Rosa Parks's mug shot. We all know what Parks did for civil rights when she refused to move to the back of the bus. But some one hundred and seventy years after Truth stood up in Akron, her own contributions have been boiled down to coasters and stamps and five words she likely never said in Ohio: "And ain't I a woman?"

But before we get there, let's start at the beginning.

★ ★ ★

SOJOURNER TRUTH WAS BORN a slave named Isabella in upstate New York's Ulster County sometime in the late 1790s. Her married slave parents were somehow able to grow old together, though their thirteen children were sold away, including Isabella herself. Surprised to hear this was in New York? We think of slavery as uniquely Southern, but it existed across the United States well into the nineteenth century. Back then, Ulster County was primarily Dutch-speaking, and Isabella spoke only Dutch until age nine, when she was sold to an English-speaking family who beat her for not understanding a language she didn't know. She carried those scars on her body for the rest of her life, just as she carried a Dutch accent into the fluent English she eventually spoke.

In 1826, per a deal with her master, Isabella declared herself free by leaving. Her master, reneging on his deal, claimed she'd run away. Isabella wouldn't have it. "I did not run away," she said later, "I walked away by daylight." She was emboldened to stroll off because she'd heard the voice of God telling her to go.

With her, Isabella carried baby Sophia— named after a sister sold away long ago—in one arm, with their belongings wrapped in a cotton handkerchief in the other, leaving her four older children behind (she had five children, not thirteen as later accounts claim). Once Sophia was weaned, she was returned to Isabella's former master. That, sickeningly, was the law. The State of New York "freed" its slaves on July 4, 1827—just months after Isabella freed herself—but to protect "property owners," a staggered system was put in place. Slaves born before 1799 were declared free immediately (Isabella just made it), but those born after had to remain "indentured servants" until age twenty-five (women) or twenty-eight (men). Leaving her children must have been heartbreaking, but Isabella heeded her God.

Seventeen years later Isabella was working as a domestic servant in New York City when the voice of God spoke to her again. She gave her employer less than an hour's notice before fleeing the "second Sodom" of the city. Setting out alone, Isabella now rechristened herself *Sojourner Truth*, a name ripe with earnest pilgrimage and verity.

Sojourner Truth began her public career as a preacher in Millennial camps. Not *that*

kind of Millennial—these ones were waiting for the end of the world and many, including Truth, welcomed it. The coming end meant some folks getting their eternal comeuppance. Like, say, slave owners and slavery sympathizers. What started as preaching began to include abolitionism and from there, women's rights. This was a familiar continuum for women abolitionists, including Lucretia Mott, Elizabeth Cady Stanton, and many others. So was preaching as precursor to other kinds of public speaking.

To be a woman addressing "promiscuous" audiences—that is, both men and women— took guts. To do it as a black woman took outright fearlessness. White men like Truth's friend Marius Robinson might be beaten and tarred by an angry mob for speaking against slavery, as he was in 1837. A black woman faced far worse. Truth had her share of scary showdowns, both with riled-up crowds and with individuals, including more than one physical assault by train conductors who felt she did not belong on public transportation. Through it all, Truth kept talking.

In 1846 she began dictating *The Narrative of Sojourner Truth* to Olive Gilbert, about whom we know little beyond her being Truth's amanuensis. Truth's memoir was likely inspired by the success of *Narrative of the Life of Frederick Douglass, an American Slave*. Unlike Douglass, who knew Truth and was notably patronizing toward her, she could neither read nor write. Again, it was her voice that made her.

★ ★ ★

TRUTH'S FAMOUS "AIN'T I A WOMAN?" is such a perfect, pithy phrase. It celebrates black and female identity. It's righteous, bald, and a little angry. I suppose it shouldn't be messed with. But mess we must. Because if ever there was a woman who fiercely believed in the sanctity of the word—the holiness of truth— it was Truth herself.

At the time she spoke in Akron, she was living nearby with Marius Robinson and his wife, Emily, who were the *Anti-Slavery Bugle*'s respective editor and publisher. It was their weekly journal that had called for the second Ohio Woman's Rights Convention, where Marius served as both a journalist covering the event and as meeting secretary, writing every- thing down as it happened there. Chair of the convention was writer and activist Frances Dana Gage, who may have taken notes when she was wasn't managing the big crowd and numerous speakers. Gage, a respected white abolitionist and suffragist, is important to this story—stay tuned.

The day after Truth spoke, Robinson summed up his feelings in the *Bugle*: "Those only can appreciate it who saw her powerful form, her whole-souled, earnest gestures, and listened to her strong and truthful tones." And then he shared Truth's speech, in full. Herewith, some of the section in question:

"I am a woman's rights. I have as much muscle as any man. I have plowed and reaped and husked and chopped and mowed, and can any man do more than that? I have heard much about the sexes being equal; I can carry as much as any man that is now. . . . The poor men seem all in confusion, and don't know what to do. Why children, if you have woman's

rights give it to her and you will feel much better. You will have your own rights, and they wont be so much trouble. I cant read, but I can hear. I have heard the bible and have learned that Eve caused man to sin. Well if woman upset the world, do give her a chance to set it right side up again."

What Truth said in the Old Stone Church mattered then, as now. It got a great reaction from the mostly white crowd, as Truth's talks usually did. She was eloquent and disarming, using humor to slip in painful points. That's what the phrase "Why children, if you have woman's rights give it to her and you will feel much better" is doing—she's chiding men and offering them a gentle out.

★ ★ ★

MISSING IN ROBINSON'S ACCOUNT is any phrase like "Ain't I a woman?" In fact, no contemporary accounts had it. The phrase—or one like it—would appear quite suddenly over a dozen years later, in 1863. That's when a new version of Truth's 1851 speech was published by the aforementioned Frances Dana Gage:

"Dat man over dar say dat woman needs to be helped into carriages, and lifted over ditches, and to have de best place eberywhar. Nobody eber helps me into carriages or ober mud-puddles, or gives me any best place . . . And ar'n't I a woman? Look at me. Look at my arm . . . I have plowed and planted and gathered into barns, and no man could head me—and ar'n't I a woman? I could work as much and eat as much as a man, (when I could get it,) and bear de lash as well—and ar'n't I a woman? I have borne thirteen chillen, and seen 'em mos' all sold off into slavery, and when I cried out with a mother's grief, none but Jesus heard—and ar'n't I a woman?"

What a difference a decade makes. Gage's version of Truth in Akron sounds nothing like Robinson's. Suddenly Truth speaks in a pronounced dialect, while repeating a new refrain: "ar'n't I a woman," which still later accounts updated to "ain't I a woman."

What I wouldn't give for a smartphone strategically placed in that Akron church or a crackly old-time recording of Truth's speech just the way she said it. Barring that, I'd bet my money on Robinson's next-day, firsthand account of a close friend whose way of talking he knew well.

Regardless, it's "Ain't I a Woman" that's stuck.

★ ★ ★

THE INDIGNITY AND APPROPRIATION

didn't begin with Gage. In 1853 Truth had visited Harriet Beecher Stowe, who "puffed" (i.e., blurbed) the newest edition of Truth's memoir, which helped boost sales. Stowe was the author of an influential little book called *Uncle Tom's Cabin*, a worldwide phenomenon that made her rich and well-traveled. She raved about Truth's charisma, which was especially notable considering she'd met Abraham Lincoln ("So you're the little woman who wrote the book that made this great war!") and was friends with Mark Twain.

Truth made such an impression on Stowe that ten years later Stowe published a popular piece in *The Atlantic Monthly* titled "Sojourner Truth, the Libyan Sibyl." Under the mistaken impression that Truth was dead, Stowe freely embellished their encounter. The main thrust of the story was Stowe taking credit for inspiring a work called *The Libyan Sibyl*, by American sculptor William Wetmore Story, a piece he considered his best. According to Stowe, it was her own descriptions of Truth (especially her voice) that moved Story to create his masterpiece ("Sojourner, singing this hymn, seemed to impersonate the fervor of Ethiopia, wild, savage, hunted of all nations, but burning after God in her tropic heart"). Story denied it, Truth was offended, and the public ate it up. Frances Dana Gage, now living with freedpeople (former slaves liberated by Union forces) in South Carolina, read Stowe's piece in *The Atlantic* and felt she had a better Sojourner Truth story. Her response, published a month later, was the so-called "Ain't I a woman?"

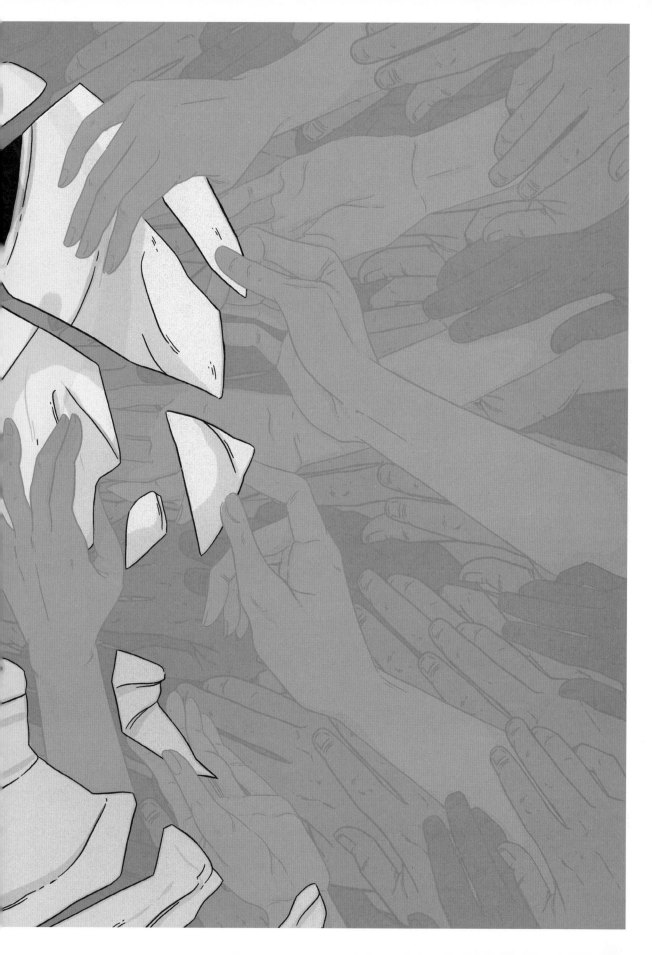

account beloved today. Gage ends her piece by explicitly correcting Stowe: "Sojourner Truth is not dead; but, old and feeble, she rests from her labors near Battle Creek, Michigan." Truth, not just alive but active for some twenty years after publication of Stowe and Gage's articles, objected to both.

In case I've pulled punches, how's this: White suffragists treated black women with little regard and certainly not as equals. History, I regret to report, shows us this again and again. Stowe and Gage made shit up. The opposite of truth. Bad, possibly worse, they appropriated Truth's voice. But they could not steal her image. Truth controlled that.

The first human voice was captured in 1860, and Thomas Edison made his first phonograph recording in 1877. But though Truth died in 1883, there's no evidence she was ever recorded. Photography, on the other hand, was already widespread in Truth's lifetime, and it was a medium she utilized brilliantly, as historian and artist Nell Irvin Painter amply demonstrates in her essential biography of Truth. As Painter points out, Truth sat for photographic portraits many times, assuming various poses, with props selected by her. Most offer variations on a theme: A serious woman simply dressed, in a demure white cap and shawl, often wearing eyeglasses and holding knitting, a book conspicuously open or nearby. Many of these details are tropes going back to traditional portrait paintings of women sewing or knitting, tasks that assert propriety and femininity. But glasses and books declare Truth's seriousness, intelligence, and even wisdom. Her first photographic portrait came within a month of Stowe's "Libyan Sibyl" article, but in her own portrayal Truth is no exotic other. She is a proper, though formidable, older woman commanding our respect. *I am a woman's rights.*

Her image lives powerfully on. Today Sojourner Truth is among the most recognized faces in America. This is in part because for nearly twenty years she circulated her *cartes-des-visite* (calling cards) widely. She earned money with them. "I sell the shadow to support the substance, Sojourner Truth" was the caption she used with her picture. "Shadow" was another word for photograph; "substance" was the woman herself. But today Truth's image is usually paired with Gage's words, "And ain't I a woman?" This is how truth is so often distorted by a history we believe we know, and too often prefer.

CHAPTER 3

ENTER ANTHONY

A discussion of the rights of animals would be regarded with far more complacency by many of what are called the wise and good of our land, than would be a discussion of the rights of woman. It is, in their estimation, to be guilty of evil thoughts, to think that woman is entitled to rights equal with man.

FREDERICK DOUGLASS, 1848

REWINDING JUST A BIT, in mid-summer 1848, Susan B. Anthony (Quaker, abolitionist, temperance activist, and schoolteacher) was in her modest sitting room in Canajoharie, New York, reading the afternoon paper when a headline caught her eye. I don't know the article Anthony actually read, but it might have gone something like:

> *WOMAN'S RIGHTS CONVENTION—A Convention dedicated to the social, civil, and religious condition of women, was held in the Wesleyan Chapel, at Seneca Falls, New York, on Wednesday and Thursday, the nineteenth and twentieth of July, commencing at ten o'clock A.M. Wednesday had been reserved for the ladies, but keen interest from both sexes meant it was a promiscuous audience who filled the church both days. Lucretia Mott, of Philadelphia, and free man Frederick Douglass, lately of Boston, among other noteworthy speakers, addressed the issue of woman in America. Most notably, Mrs. Henry Stanton of Seneca Falls held forth a document to the assembled for ratification, beginning with not little fervor, "We hold these truths to be self-evident: That all men and women are created equal."*

I like to picture Anthony reading about the astonishing and unanticipated three hundred people waiting outside; the church key that could not be found, requiring Cady Stanton to boost her nephew through a window so he could let in the crowd; the curious male partners whose milling outside the door compelled organizers to invite them in.

Anthony likely raised an eyebrow at that bit—a cadre of men who would *not* bar their wives, sisters, daughters from debating the rights of women. Who would in fact join the discussion. Presumably most of those men had their usual weekday work to attend to, but were setting it aside to hear about women's rights.

★ ★ ★

ONE OF THOSE GOOD MEN, and the most essential, was Frederick Douglass. Tall, handsome, and just a decade out of slavery, he was a bestselling author and a famous (and well-paid) orator in an age when speech-giving was king. His participation at Seneca Falls gave legitimacy to "The Hen Convention," otherwise comprised, as summarized by one newspaper, of "divorced wives, childless women, and some old maids." Not *real* women, in other words. Certainly not the sort anyone cared about.

The second day of the convention, July 20, an even larger crowd assembled, including more men. And yet, when the Declaration of Rights and Sentiments was read that day—beginning with that line tweaking the Declaration of Independence—the assembled men and women unanimously approved it.

Then the eleven resolutions were put up for a vote. Each one passed easily, until the ninth, the one written solely by Cady Stanton: "Resolved, that it is the duty of the women of this country to secure to themselves their sacred right to the elective franchise."

This one was a tougher sell. Women voting disrupted the cherished belief in "separate spheres." That is, that men and women ruled distinct—but equal!—realms of life. No surprise, the male sphere was public while

the female was domestic. If a woman wanted something done in the public sphere—voting, say, or warmongering, or earning money—her husband or father or brother did it for her. If a man wanted something done in the domestic realm—childbirth or -rearing, cooking, cleaning, clothes-making, chamber pot emptying, nursing of the ill and elderly—then women did that for him. Such balance was so obvious, ideal, and harmonious that separate spheres seemed a kind of natural law. Asking for it to be otherwise was therefore unnatural.

Henry Stanton, husband of Elizabeth Cady, had skipped town to avoid any contamination with resolution number nine. Lucretia Mott and her husband, James, who was chairing the convention (even these women weren't quite ready to trust women wholly with leadership), weren't into said resolution either. The ninth

resolution might not have passed at all had not Douglass stood in support: "In this denial of the right to participate in government, not merely the degradation of women and the perpetuation of great injustice happens, but the maiming and repudiation of one-half of the moral and intellectual power of the government of the world." The moral authority of a once enslaved, now towering free man of letters carried the day. By evening all eleven resolutions were passed. The fight was on for women's suffrage. It would be a long one, generations long.

Of some three hundred people in attendance, only a third signed the Declaration (women signed the document itself, while men signed a separate sheet as endorsement). Douglass was the only known African American signer. Only one signatory, Charlotte

Woodward Pierce, would live to see ratification of the Nineteenth Amendment in 1920, though she wasn't the youngest in attendance. I note with pleasure that the youngest person to sign the Declaration of Rights and Sentiments was fourteen-year-old Susan Quinn, representing a new wave of immigrants from Ireland. No relation that I know of, but, coincidentally, 1848 was the year my own Irish family arrived in America.

★ ★ ★

DESPITE GETTING THE THRILLING highlights in her Canajoharie sitting room, Susan B. Anthony set the newspaper aside. She was mostly unimpressed, though she had perked up a bit at the mention of Frederick Douglass, a frequent guest at her father's home in Rochester. If Douglass thought women's rights worthwhile, maybe there was something to it.

I imagine Anthony lifting her plain but tasteful tea cup, then lowering it, lost in thought. She'd given up sugar, along with cotton, in protest of the slave labor engaged in producing such items. Abolition and temperance, those were her battlefields. Her contribution to women was fighting the devil liquor and what it made men do: squander their paychecks, hit their wives, neglect their children. Women would be free when their husbands and fathers and brothers behaved. But as for the rights of women, future patron saint of women's suffrage Susan B. Anthony was more interested in what was for dinner.

Anthony was born in 1820, one of seven children, to parents who did not believe in toys ("distraction from the inner light") but did believe boys and girls were equals before God. So it annoyed grade-school Anthony when boys in her class were taught long division while she wasn't. According to Anthony, her male teacher—most teachers were men—had explained, "A girl needs to know how to read her Bible and count her egg money, nothing more." Her supportive father took her out of public school and sent her to Quaker boarding school.

Once a successful factory owner, Anthony's father went bankrupt in 1837 after some bad land deals. To support her now struggling family, Anthony became a teacher and was outraged to discover her male colleagues made more than she did. It seems strange she was surprised, since we live with obvious pay disparity almost two centuries later, but Anthony may have felt immune to the worst sexism. She was an independent working woman. She had no husband to answer to, no children to mind. She was unmarried by choice, a state she called "single blessedness." Though she had suitors as a young woman, Anthony turned them all away. "I never felt I could give up my freedom to become a man's housekeeper," she said.

But Susan B. Anthony was slow to come aboard the women's suffrage movement. She did not attend a second women's rights convention held two weeks after Seneca Falls, in Rochester, though her parents and two sisters were there and signed a document of resolutions that again included support for the women's vote.

In fact, Anthony had no particular interest in women's rights at all until a fateful encounter on a Seneca Falls street corner in May 1851, two years later.

She was staying with friend and fellow temperance crusader Amelia Bloomer, a journalist who had attended the Seneca Falls Convention and had recently launched a paper called *The Lily*. It would be instrumental in spreading the gospel of women's rights and in championing a liberating clothing style that became synonymous with its editor (more on that in Chapter 5). Anthony was out with Bloomer for an afternoon constitutional and a bit of spring air. I imagine the fateful day as wet, probably muddy. Anthony, always neat as a pin, holding up her skirt to avoid any mess. Then Bloomer spotted Elizabeth Cady Stanton, skirt likely dragging as she was ringed by her young sons. Bloomer raised a gloved hand, hailing Cady Stanton, and made introductions. There began one of the greatest partnerships in American history. In the following century Anthony would write, "It is fifty-one years since we first met, and we have been busy through every one of them, stirring up the world to recognize the rights of women."

Outwardly, they seemed an odd pair. Cady Stanton, upbeat and fat, with curls that framed her broad face, and serious Anthony, tall and bony, her hair pulled back in a severe bun. At first glance they might strike us as the Abbott and Costello of women's history, but in fact they were the Marx and Engels, a pair of dangerous plotters cooking up revolution.

Elizabeth—older, married, richer, better known—said later of meeting the woman who would be her lifelong friend and fellow firebrand, "There she stood with her good,

earnest face and genial smile, dressed in gray delaine, hat and all the same color relieved with pale-blue ribbons, the perfection of neatness and sobriety. I liked her thoroughly from the beginning."

Anthony must've been moved by Cady Stanton, too, as she happily abandoned teaching to become the most visible leader in the fight for women's suffrage in America. She traveled tirelessly for decades, coast to coast, by horse and train and eventually by car, sleeping in small back bedrooms, on trains, and in boarding houses, often sharing a bed with acolytes. Anthony was surrounded by adoring and energetic young women, who affectionately called her "Aunt Susan." Lest we read too much into this bed-sharing, or even the ardor-filled letters that went back and forth between Anthony and "Susan's nieces," such romantic friendships were not uncommon in nineteenth-century America. There's no evidence that Anthony was a lesbian (though no evidence she wasn't either).

Once she started speaking out for suffrage, Anthony never stopped. Cady Stanton was the speech writer and theoretician. Anthony was her mouthpiece. Or as Cady Stanton, always an excellent wordsmith, put it, "I forged the thunderbolts, she fired them."

★ ★ ★

APPEARING BEFORE OFTEN HOSTILE CROWDS, Anthony was called "an ungainly hermaphrodite, part male, part female with an ugly face and shrill voice" (ah yes, shrillness, the usual complaint when women speak up) and "a spinster who knows nothing of marriage

and shouldn't talk about it," among more demeaning and dehumanizing things. She was threatened, she was bullied, she was hung in effigy on multiple occasions. She was tireless and incredibly brave, no question.

When Cady Stanton and Anthony teamed up, it was as a fighting force. Anthony was sometimes called "Little Napoleon," a fierce and tenacious fighter willing to die on whatever hill she deemed necessary. She spent decades on the road. Her health suffered, she was exhausted, she went on. She became famous for her commitment, energy, and unflagging drive. Her name became so inextricably linked with winning the vote for women that popular shorthand for the Nineteenth Amendment was the "Susan B. Anthony Amendment."

Cady Stanton, by contrast, was a mother of, eventually, seven children, and therefore tied to home, much to Anthony's irritation. She couldn't fathom why her friend risked so much again and again—childbirth and child-rearing—for just a "moments pleasure to herself or her husband." It also meant more work for Anthony, since she was often called into service holding the baby and entertaining children while Cady Stanton wrote.

★ ★ ★

When the Civil War broke out in April 1861, suffragists put aside politics to support the Union. No women's rights conventions took place during the four years of the war, but women were central to the war effort. The idea of an organized nurses' corps came from one of America's first women physicians,

Dr. Elizabeth Blackwell. Nursing had been a male profession (that's how Walt Whitman spent the war), but women now took up the grisly battlefield occupation. Clara Barton helped create an agency of women nurses, including the author Louisa May Alcott. Other women sewed bandages and made various medical supplies. This was all essential work, of course, but many women likely shared Alcott's feeling: "If I was only a boy I'd march off tomorrow." Nursing offered plenty of danger, by the way, if not from cannon fire then from disease. Alcott herself contracted typhoid and nearly died of it.

Stanton's two oldest sons served as soldiers, as did two sons of Douglass. Truth's grandson and Anthony's brother fought for the Union. They all believed, fervently, in the rightness of their cause and in the abolition of slavery.

When Lincoln issued the Emancipation Proclamation in 1863, stating that all slaves held in states "then in rebellion against the United States, shall be then, thenceforward, and forever free," suffragists celebrated. And when the war ended in 1865—hooray!—and the Thirteenth Amendment was ratified soon after (stating that "Neither slavery nor involuntary servitude, except as a punishment for crime whereof the party shall have been duly convicted, shall exist within the United States, or any place subject to their jurisdiction."), the early suffragists, led by Elizabeth Cady Stanton and Susan B. Anthony, threw up their arms in victory.

And then.

Reconstruction. In 1868, the Fourteenth Amendment was ratified, saying everyone who was a citizen—born one, naturalized, or former slave—had "equal protection of the law." This should have been great news for everyone. But the Fourteenth Amendment also inserted the first mention of gender into the U.S. Constitution, saying all *male* citizens over twenty-one had the right to vote. For the first time, the Constitution codified two distinct classes of citizens, based on sex: male and female.

Then in 1870, the Fifteenth Amendment said that the aforementioned right to vote could not be denied on the basis of "race, color, or previous condition of servitude." Meaning that in this very opportunity to open the door to women, only black men were welcomed inside. Women were left out in the cold. With this, many suffragists lost their shit, including and especially Cady Stanton and Anthony. And I mean that. They lost their minds. Former abolitionists, *friends* of Frederick Douglass, Cady Stanton and Anthony made terrible, disgusting remarks, sometimes with Douglass in the audience.

Cady Stanton said things like, "Now, as the celestial gate to civil rights is slowly moving on its hinges, it becomes a serious question whether we had better stand aside and see 'Sambo' walk into the kingdom first." When Douglass objected, Anthony struck back, "If you will not give the whole loaf of suffrage to the entire people, give it to the most intelligent first." Inveighing against the vote being given to black men and incoming immigrants before women, Cady Stanton railed about

"Patrick and Sambo and Hans and Yung Tung" and wrote, "The best interests of the nation demand that we outweigh this incoming pauperism, ignorance, and degradation with the wealth, education, and refinement of the women of the republic." It was racist, nativist, sickening, and not the first, or the last, time Anthony and Cady Stanton would ally themselves with bigotry.

In 1867, Kansas proposed amending the state constitution to remove "white" and "male" from state voting qualifications. This would, obviously, pave the way for black and women's suffrage in the state. Suffrage activists rushed in, including Cady Stanton and Anthony. Things took increasingly grim turns as they allied themselves with a wealthy pro-slavery dandy named George Train, who financed their cause while tossing off such

charming bon mots as, "Woman first, and negro last, is my programme."

They shrugged off Train's obvious racism in hopes of winning the "woman first" part.

Longtime abolitionist and fervent supporter of women's rights William Lloyd Garrison called Train "crack-brained, harlequin, and semi-lunatic," while Cady Stanton waxed about his being "the most wonderful man of the century in some respects." In pursuit of a just cause—the vote for women—Cady Stanton and Anthony had seized on the tactic of the desperate: the ends justifying the means. The road to hell is paved with good intentions.

In response, Lucretia Mott reluctantly split with her old friends; she could no longer abide their appalling tactics. Other important leaders, such as Lucy Stone, went further.

Stone spearheaded a total schism in the movement, creating an independent organization entirely apart from Anthony and Cady Stanton. It was now the American Woman Suffrage Association (AWSA), led by Stone, versus the National Woman Suffrage Association (NWSA) led by Cady Stanton and Anthony. The NWSA opposed the Fifteenth Amendment, while the AWSA promoted its ratification, even if it meant women would need to wait. And wait they would.

CHAPTER 4

WINNING THE WEST: SACAJAWEA

In general, western women remain the orphans of women's history.

JOAN HOFF WILSON
MONTANA: THE MAGAZINE OF WESTERN HISTORY

IN 1905, SUSAN B. ANTHONY arrived in Portland, Oregon, by motorcar. I picture her pulling up a little dusty and puckered, inching out of a cramped backseat and slowly unfolding. No surprise if she was a little rattled. Eighty-six years old, she'd been hustling for the vote for more than half a century. She'd seen some progress, too. In fifty-some years of campaigning, four states had granted women "full" suffrage (meaning local, state, and national voting rights), all in the West: Wyoming (1890); Colorado (1893); and Utah and Idaho (1896). It wouldn't have surprised Anthony that the next half dozen states to go for suffrage would likewise be Western ones: Washington (1910); California (1911); Oregon, Kansas, and Arizona (1912); and Montana (1914).

The purpose of Anthony's 1905 visit to Portland was in fact twofold: suffrage and Sacajawea.

The thirty-seventh National American Woman Suffrage Association Convention was being held in Portland that summer. In 1890, after two decades of schism, the AWSA and NWSA had reunited to form NAWSA as a united front in the fight for suffrage. Anthony, NAWSA's honorary president, was there for the closing benediction. It was her third trip in thirty years to Oregon, where women's voting rights had been rejected twice and were up for decision again in 1906. They would lose a third time. Oregon men denied female suffrage five times, more than any other state (though even that delay didn't stop them from being the seventh state in the Union to approve a woman's right to vote).

The Oregon women of 1905 didn't know that yet, and they'd plotted out what they thought would be a very convincing political double-punch. The NAWSA meeting deliberately coincided with another major Portland event, a kind of unofficial world's fair, the Lewis and Clark Centennial Exposition. Centerpiece of the months-long celebration was the unveiling and dedication of a heroic-size bronze statue, *Sacajawea and Jean-Baptiste*. On a pedestal of rough-hewn stone illustrative of the arduous path she'd trod for thousands of miles, Sacajawea strides forward, right arm raised toward the Oregon coast, baby Jean-Baptiste snug against her back. He peeks winningly over her shoulder, while her loose wrap whips at her sides like the wings of an Indigenous angel. More than a simple portrait of Sacajawea and her son, the statue is inspiring and aspirational.

Sacajawea had only recently become a popular part of the Lewis and Clark story. This was thanks to an Oregon novelist named Eva Emery Dye, who uncovered an enduring symbol for American women by imaginatively retelling the remarkable story of a young Shoshone badass in her 1902 historical novel, *The Conquest: The True Story of Lewis and Clark*. Dye's novel, a big seller in its day, had given Western suffragists a bronze-worthy heroine.

I could go on and on about the awesomeness of a teenager who took part in one of the greatest adventures in human history as one of the youngest members of the Corps of Discovery, the only Native, and only woman. She also gave birth just two months before joining the expedition, then carried her baby some seven thousand miles over the Continental Divide to the Pacific Ocean and back again. You know how they say Ginger

Rogers did everything Fred Astaire did, but backward in heels? Sacajawea did everything Lewis and Clark did, with another human being on her back.

All this resonated with suffragists in the West, many of whom could remember pioneer hardships, Rocky Mountain winters, and the strength of their mothers and grandmothers. They were inspired by Sacajawea's fortitude as both a Corps member and a mother. It ran counter to the hysteria promoted by the anti-suffrage camp: that if women voted babies would suffer. Who would watch the children if women were loose in the world?! Not only did Sacajawea carry her son while braving lightning, hail, and grizzly bears; calmly save vital equipment from a capsizing canoe while saving herself and her child; point out Bozeman Pass as the ideal place to cross

the Continental Divide; and provide essential communication with plains tribes; in addition to all that, she also—hang on to your hats—voted. In Oregon.

When the Corps arrived where the Columbia River meets the Pacific Ocean, the captains called for a vote to decide where to spend winter. Sacajawea's vote, along with that of York, the only black member of the Corps, were counted the same as those cast by the white men. The Corps voted to spend the winter of 1805–06 near today's Astoria, Oregon, where they built Fort Clatsop.

In addition to promoting Sacajawea as heroine and early voter, Dye wrote, "Some day, upon the Bozeman Pass, Sacajawea's statue will stand beside that of Clark." Soon after the book's publication, Dye became president of the Sacajawea Statue Association, which raised

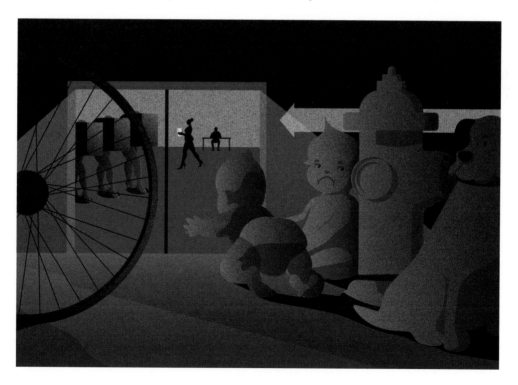

thousands to create a worthy monument and selected its sculptor. They chose Denver artist Alice Cooper (not *that* Alice Cooper, obviously), who utilized some twenty tons of copper to excellent effect. And that's what eighty-six-year-old Susan B. Anthony was in Oregon to dedicate in 1905.

★ ★ ★

THIS IS NOTHING SHORT OF A MIRACLE.

Sacajawea died uncelebrated and unknown. So unremarkable that after returning to St. Louis with the rest of the Lewis and Clark expedition, she simply disappears from history. Natives and historians dispute the date and place of her death, from 1812 (age twenty-four) to 1885 (age ninety-seven). Maybe she died in North Dakota, or it could have been Wyoming. No one knows how to spell her name, either, or how to say it.

Yet, as a kid growing up in 1970s Montana, I knew more about Sacajawea than I did about, say, George Washington. I saw paintings, posters, and sculptures with her image, saw her name on streets, schools, and springs. I knew she'd camped near my childhood home while portaging the big falls of the Missouri. Thanks to Dye, the suffragist movement, and the West's appreciation for (or maybe just its desperate need for) independent women, Sacajawea was my first girl idol.

★ ★ ★

Back in Portland 1905, Susan B. Anthony made her slow way across the exposition

plaza to the statue of Sacajawea in its center and unfolded her speech. "We pay homage to thousands of uncrowned heroines," she began. On this day, like many days in her long life, Anthony expressed admiration for the power of women everywhere. She did believe all women deserved the same rights as men, regardless of race and class, though she did not believe black men should get the vote before women. And like generals of audacious campaigns throughout history, she was ruthless in pursuit of victory.

Eight months later she'd enter history herself. Anthony passed away in March 1906 from pneumonia and heart failure, and was immediately crowned the patron saint of women's suffrage.

In 1979, as recognition, Jimmy Carter approved the minting of the Susan B. Anthony dollar, the first American money to bear the image of a real woman (rather than, say, Lady Liberty). Nobody liked it. Small and silver, easily mixed up with quarters, the Susan B. Anthony dollar's production lasted less than three years, though it was briefly revived in 1999. It was replaced in 2000 with the "golden dollar," a brass-clad coin bearing the image of Sacajawea. Not in traditional profile but turning mid-stride, a woman of action with a baby asleep on her back.

CHAPTER 5

BLOOMERS, BICYCLES & BASKETBALL

Let me tell you what I think of bicycling. I think it has done more to emancipate women than anything else in the world.

SUSAN B. ANTHONY, 1896

They were more than a skilled basketball team. They were a rare gathering of young female warriors.

TURTLE WOMAN (JESSIE JAMES-HAWLEY), 2001, ON THE 1904 WORLD CHAMPIONS OF BASKETBALL

PERSONALLY, WHEN I THINK of bloomers, I conjure can-can girls at the Moulin Rouge in 1890s Paris kicking up their legs so *les gens* in the back can get a gander at poofy white pants and, squinting, imagine what's hiding underneath. Not a fashion accessory with obvious associations to women's emancipation.

But originally, bloomers were distinctly feminist in design and intention, related to the movement known as "dress reform" or sometimes the "rational dress movement." Reform was unquestionably needed.

American fashion of the 1850s—even in out-of-the-way places like Seneca Falls—demanded that women cinch their waists in tightly laced corsets with whalebone stays and then layer on up to eight petticoats, long enough to drag on the ground. This protected women's modesty while creating a pleasing hourglass shape. This also deformed organs, made breathing difficult, and rendered free movement almost impossible, as all those petticoats weighed up to fifteen pounds. Walking upstairs was challenging, forget hiking up a hill. Going to the bathroom was ridiculous. Pregnancy, a nightmare.

But in the early 1850s, a woman named Elizabeth Smith Miller, a relation of Elizabeth Cady Stanton, arrived on the scene sporting pants under a shortened skirt. Originally called "Turkish" dress, it was outrageous by American standards of contemporary womanhood, as it offended both fashion and decency. But the outfit immediately made sense to Cady Stanton, who'd seen Haudenosaunee women wearing tunics over leggings her whole life. Native women planted, reaped, rode, and enjoyed physical freedoms most non-Native

"As soon as it became known that I was wearing the new dress, letters came pouring in upon me by hundreds of women all over the country asking for patterns," Bloomer wrote. As for the *The Lily*, the newfangled threads were so aligned with the newspaper's mission of encouraging women's liberation that a pattern for sewing one's own pair came free with all new subscriptions. Circulation jumped from 500 copies per month to 4,000. Women wearing the new style were called Bloomerites, or were said to be adherents of Bloomerism. In time, the new fashion was simply called "bloomers," after their vocal proponent.

Wearing bloomers in the 1850s was a little like sporting a fan mohawk in the 1970s, a wordless public signal declaring yourself a certain kind of rebel. Which also made wearing them dangerous. Women in bloomers were subject to constant street harassment, from name-calling to worse, and though many of the early suffragists adopted the fashion, public speakers like Anthony grew wary when her attire got far more press than what she had to say (paging Hillary Clinton).

women never could in their fabric prisons of dragging skirts and constricting corsets.

In the April 1851 edition of her feminist paper, *The Lily*, an excited Amelia Bloomer—the journalist who introduced Cady Stanton and Anthony—promoted the new shortened skirt and pants combo to her readers in terms both celebratory and sinister. "The health of untold thousands has been sacrificed, and countless numbers of fair and lovely beings have committed suicide and gone down to early graves," she warned of current female fashion. Hyperbole? Hard to say. But what's incontrovertible is that not unlike stiletto heels, corsets and heavy skirts meant women were barely mobile. They couldn't easily walk, work, ride a horse, or do anything that required movement, deep breathing, sweat, and stamina. They could not run away.

Cady Stanton's own son begged her not to wear bloomers when she visited him at boarding school. *Harper's* ridiculed them, etc. Eventually, Cady Stanton and Anthony and even Amelia Bloomer herself reluctantly gave them up. But only for a time. By 1890, the controversial "under" pants were back, paired with the bicycle to give women a heady dose of physical emancipation: legs moving, heart pumping, hair coming undone.Freedom!

By the 1890s bicycling was a nationwide craze, in part because the new "safety bicycle" was much easier to ride than earlier versions.

But only if women wore bloomers. In a dress, a bike could be downright deadly. An 1896 letter to the British *Daily Press* wrote with regret of the death of a Miss Carr, who had her feet "in the rests" on a descent and when she attempted to return them to their proper position, "she could not see the pedals, as the flapping skirt hid them from her view, and she had to fumble for them. Could she have taken but a momentary glance at their position, she would have had a good chance to save her life."

Shake off those dusty bloomers, ladies.

(Though, as a crucial aside, bloomers could not protect women from a now-rare malady that apparently afflicted nineteenth-century women, called "bicycle face." Commentators warned that bicycling might strike a young woman ugly at any moment, with no warning. Ominously, it was said to sometimes be permanent. Regardless, women cycled on.)

From one sport to the next, it turned out bloomers were ideal for all sorts of vigorous activities, from bicycling to swimming (yikes), and, a personal favorite: basket ball (as originally spelled).

★ ★ ★

INVENTED IN DECEMBER 1891 by Canadian physician and PE teacher James Naismith, basket ball was an indoor, less painful answer to football. It caught on immediately for both sexes.

As early as 1896 the first women's intercollegiate game was played in San Francisco, between Stanford and Berkeley, to a packed crowd of some seven hundred women spectators. To preserve the players' modesty, men were banned, since players were running up and down court in sweaters and bloomers, perspiring and jumping and who knows what. (One can only imagine the titillation.) Some intrepid men climbed the outside of the building to peer in through windows near the roof, forcing women inside to fend them off with sticks.

Stanford won, by the way, but that didn't stop the school from soon banning women's basketball for the next seven decades "for the good of the students' health." Similarly, California men voted down giving women the vote just months after the celebrated first women's collegiate basketball game in their state.

California Men 2—Women in Bloomers 0.

Things weren't going much better for basketball at all-women Smith College, across the country. Letters home raved about the fabulous new game on campus. To the concern of parents. Who consulted doctors. Who confirmed their worst fears: Basketball was incredibly dangerous! (When my mother played five decades later, there was still some concern about a woman's uterus falling right out of her body.)

To keep her sport on campus, Smith's PE teacher, Senda Berenson, developed "girls' rules" basketball. This removed much of the running and other physical aspects of the game (fighting over the ball, dribbling, using the full court, etc.). In this way she appeased parents and concerned faculty, and "saved" basketball at Smith.

Despite those early hiccups, the original game ("boys' rules") was spreading, and in some schools—especially those out West—both genders embraced the game of speed and aggression we play today. Some understood the sport's demands better than others. Some were born to it. Say, for example, the Native women of the Fort Shaw Government Industrial Indian Boarding School, the first World Champions of Basketball.

FOUNDED IN LATE 1892, Montana's Fort Shaw Boarding School was situated on vast prairie land. On a clear day you might see more than a hundred miles in any direction, if you could hike to the top of Square Butte, a towering rectilinear formation rising abruptly from the plains a few acres outside the school. The school's three hundred students came from ancient people. The ancestors of the Blackfeet

students, for example, had run buffalo off nearby Ulm Pishkun all the way back to at least 500 CE.

Josephine Langley was the Fort Shaw girls' coach and Blackfeet herself. She felt certain her students would take to basketball, maybe because in many plains tribes—Shoshone and Cree, for example—girls traditionally played a fast-paced, competitive game called double ball. Langley understood her students' homesickness for their families and tribes, and knew how desperate they were to maintain their own Native cultures. If you don't know about the Bureau of Indian Affairs schools, here's the quote most widely associated with their pedagogical approach: "Kill the Indian in him, and save the man."

A teacher like Langley was a treasure. And she was right about her students' passion for basketball.

On Thanksgiving Day 1902, the Fort Shaw women played their first big game, against the women of Butte High, a public high school in what was then Montana's biggest city. The auditorium overflowed with hundreds of rowdy local fans. Over on the Fort Shaw bench, they would have witnessed a team of Native teenagers in matching handmade wool serge uniforms, comprised of loose-fitting bloomers that came just below the knees and matching long-sleeved middies with wide sailor-style square collars. The middy shirts were worn over striped dickeys (a rather nautical theme for landlocked Montana) and monogrammed with a big F on the left side and an S on the right. The uniforms ended in cotton stockings and leather gym shoes the Fort Shaw boys had made in shoemaking class.

All this was, naturally, just as lightweight, cool, and breathable as it sounds. How they did not die of heatstroke is a miracle (let's not even discuss the weight and smell of wet wool), but it was Montana and basketball is a winter sport. Maybe it was all quite manageable. Fort Shaw beat Butte.

In fact, they beat most all the teams in Montana in those outfits—including men's teams and women's college teams—and were named unofficial state champs. And the streak earned them an invitation to the Louisiana Purchase Exposition in St. Louis, otherwise known as the 1904 World's Fair. That's summer. In the Midwest. There was no time or money for new uniforms, so off they went in wool.

Women have for too long been anonymous in history, so herewith the World's Fair Fort Shaw team: Minnie Burton (Shoshone); Nettie Wirth (Assiniboine); Emma Sansaver (Métis and Chippewa-Cree); Belle Johnson (Piegan Blackfeet); Genie Butch (Assiniboine); Genevieve Healy (Gros Ventre); Katie Snell (Gros Ventre); Sarah Mitchell (Assiniboine-Chippewa and Shoshone); Rose LaRose (Shoshone); Flora Lucero (Chippewa-Cree). They lived together, studied together, and played basketball together. They were seamless in their speed and teamwork.

Over the first two weeks of June, 1904, Fort Shaw played all comers at train stops from Great Falls to St. Louis, before setting foot on the grounds of the 1904 World's Fair at last, only to be informed that the local St. Louis team—older and comprised of handpicked alumni from the best women's teams across the state—was undefeated and confident they could take an Indian team from a tiny Montana town.

Fort Shaw didn't have time to worry. The game against the St. Louis "all-stars" was preceded by a rigorous schedule of exhibition games for fair visitors all through the hot summer. Geronimo, the legendary Apache chief who was also a fair participant, liked to watch. As did the coach of the St. Louis team, who used what he saw to train his own women.

But when they finally played Fort Shaw that fall, in a best of three series, St. Louis no-showed once and lost twice, badly. The women of Fort Shaw were crowned champions of the 1904 World's Fair, with an accompanying silver trophy. According to journalists, especially the Montana press, a women's team had been crowned the first World Champions of Basketball.

★ ★ ★

Within three years, none of the Fort Shaw women still played. They'd married mostly and among them would have sixty-two children. Sarah Mitchell had eleven. Emma Sansaver, mother of nine, ran a ranch with her husband outside Havre, near the Canadian border. A photo shows her there astride a chestnut mare, two white horses held lightly by the reigns in her right hand. In addition to a cowboy hat and neckerchief, she's wearing her old team uniform, the F and S still evident on the square collar of her middy blouse. Sitting tall in the saddle in her old team bloomers, Sansaver stares evenly at the camera, a woman of action in repose, comfortable and confident.

CHAPTER 6

THE ART OF PROTEST: MARY CASSATT VS. THE ANTIS

Speak to me of France. Women do not have to fight for recognition here if they do serious work.

MARY CASSATT, AMERICAN IMPRESSIONIST IN PARIS

NO WOMAN HAS A RIGHT TO DRAW LIKE THAT.

EDGAR DEGAS, FRENCH IMPRESSIONIST

POOR MARY CASSATT. She spent most of her headstrong life as an independent woman abroad, working alongside the bad boys of the Paris avant-garde—Edgar Degas, Édouard Manet, Auguste Renoir, Camille Pissarro. But we tend to think of her as a lady artist who painted sweet mothers and babies, women in white dresses, small children. Soft. Sentimental. *Feminine*.

Not long ago I posted something about Cassatt's badassery on Facebook and an Ivy-educated friend was quick to respond, "Really? So interesting. You'd never know from her demure women!" But as I've written elsewhere, art can be dangerous, even when decorous. Often deliberately so.

And what we now sometimes see as saccharine—Impressionism itself, say— was shocking in its time, often for reasons

that would surprise us. Take Cassatt's mural *Modern Woman*, created for the Woman's Building at the 1893 World's Columbian Exposition in Chicago. Designed by MIT graduate Sophia Hayden, the Woman's Building was an entirely female affair, with statuary by San Francisco sculptor Alice Rideout and caryatids by Enid Yandell, a student of Rodin. Cassatt, who'd been exhibiting in Paris for over twenty years, was in a different league from them. But she was eager to plant a foot back in American artistic soil. She also liked the idea of a building created by and dedicated to women.

Situated in a vast interior courtyard, Cassatt's mural was monumental in ambition and size, about sixty feet long and fourteen feet at its highest. It consisted of three panels, which show women pursuing (left to right)

Fame, Knowledge, and Art. The largest scene, *Young Women Plucking the Fruits of Knowledge and Science*, filled a massive center lunette. Depicting contemporary women in an apple orchard, it's ostensibly tame stuff. But the Tree of Knowledge of Good and Evil, and its fruit, appears in the Bible and in Western art for thousands of years with women depicted as the agents of man's fall from grace. Cassatt's painting doesn't include men at all. Women pluck apples and pass them down to younger girls, one generation feeding another the wholesome fruits of their own labor.

If her repositioning of women as virtuous harvesters of the tree of knowledge was a gentle takedown, it still upset people. As Cassatt relayed in a letter: "An American friend asked me in a rather huffy tone the other day, 'Then this is woman apart from her relations to man!' I told him it was. Men I have no doubt are painted in all their vigor on the walls of other buildings."

For most women in Chicago, the Woman's Building was a big hit. In the building's six months of existence, more than 200,000 women saw Cassatt's mural, including suffragists like Susan B. Anthony and her young supporter Carrie Chapman Catt (more on her to come). Women praised it, but critics shook their heads. Cassatt's subject, sniffed one, "seems too trivial and below the dignity of the great occasion." When the building came down at the end of the fair, her mural was put in storage, and from there it just disappeared. No one knows what became of the only monumental artwork created by one of America's most significant artists.

★ ★ ★

AMERICA NEVER KNEW what it had with Cassatt. Raised mostly in Philadelphia, in middling high society, Cassatt first studied art in Paris in 1865. By 1874 she was there for good, because Paris was the center of the art world. French opinion was what mattered to her. She'd lose most other things. In 1882, her beloved sister Lydia passed away in her sleep. Cassatt was bereft. She'd eschewed marriage for art, but had imagined a future with her sister, the two of them independent women abroad doing what they will. Her feminist interpretation of Eden—women relying on other women—was engraved on her heart.

Lydia was her companion and her older (by seven years) chaperone. Although Mary Cassatt could not in any case frequent cafes or nightlife venues as male Impressionists did, she could at least, together with Lydia, attend the theater, the opera, the Louvre. When she lost her sister, Cassatt lost friendship and freedom. She also lost a willing model.

One reason Cassatt painted so many scenes of women reading, knitting, drinking tea, and minding children was that these were the private spaces allowed her as a woman. By depicting such humble environments she elevated scenes of women's work, pastimes, friendships, and occupations as worthy of high art. Others were unpersuaded, including her friend Edgar Degas who, on seeing her 1899 painting *Mother and Child (The Oval Mirror)*, proclaimed it, "The greatest picture of the nineteenth century . . . It is the little Jesus and his English nurse."

Degas was famous for his sarcasm, just as Cassatt was known for her hot temper and sharp tongue. They had regular fallings-out, but admired and supported each other's work. Degas had invited Cassatt into the Impressionist circle, but she was never his student, a myth that persists. They were collaborators and friends, assessing each other's work, sharing enthusiasm for Japanese prints, bartering artworks, and giving each other shit. She once complained to her friend Louisine Havemeyer, "You don't know what a dreadful man he is, he can say anything." Havemeyer shot back: "So can you."

★ ★ ★

BY THE TURN OF THE CENTURY, Cassatt's reputation was thriving in France. In 1904 she was named a Chevalier of the *Légion d'Honneur.* American artists in Paris sought her blessing and advice, wealthy Americans sought her discerning eye and connections. But it was her brother Aleck, president of the Pennsylvania Railroad from 1899 to 1906, who was famous in America.

Cassatt loved her brothers and their families, but on visits to France they tried her patience. She wanted to be a good aunt and sister, going so far as to travel to Egypt with her brother Gardner's family in 1910. Which was a mistake. Gardner took ill and died soon after his return. Cassatt was devastated by his death, as well as crushed by the masculine intensity of Egyptian art. Sick physically and spiritually, she could barely work.

Reenter longtime friend Louisine Havemeyer, who came for an extended visit

in 1914. A wealthy widow, avid art collector, and powerhouse suffragist, Havemeyer was active in the Women's Political Union in New York, headed by Harriot Stanton Blatch (daughter of Elizabeth Cady Stanton), and an ally of radical suffragist Alice Paul.

On long afternoon walks, Havemeyer and Cassatt discussed everything that was wrong in the world and how they would fix it. Women's suffrage was essential. "If the world is to be saved, it will be the women who save it," Cassatt agreed. I like to picture them hiking the hilly countryside in their big hats and long skirts. Cassatt thin and walking with a cane, Havemeyer energetic and sure-footed, both of them gray-haired and elegant, a living Impressionist picture. And like Impressionism, though offering a pretty picture, these dames were rebels cackling beneath their parasols.

In 1912 Havemeyer had thrown a successful double bill, an El Greco/Goya show, to raise money for suffrage. She decided she'd do it again with a modern master: Degas. But she realized a suffrage exhibit without a woman artist was wrongheaded. (Yes.) She asked if Cassatt would join Degas. More than willing, Cassatt liked the idea of poking a feminist finger in Degas's patriarchal eye.

★ ★ ★

LIKE HER WOMAN'S BUILDING MURAL

of 1893, Cassatt's quiet paintings of mothers and children in Havemeyer's 1915 suffrage show were unlikely incendiaries. But what was left of Cassatt's family—Aleck and his wife and children, as well as Gardner's widow, Jennie, and her two daughters, with

whom she'd traveled on the fateful trip to Egypt—all disavowed the exhibition. They'd become fiercely anti-suffragist activists in a well-funded nationwide movement of self-proclaimed "Antis." The extended Cassatt family marshaled their considerable finances against votes for women. And they attempted to thwart their sister and aunt.

The suffrage exhibition in New York depended on borrowed paintings from private collections. Cassatt's family had much of her best early work, which they refused to lend. Other collectors followed their lead. Cassatt was forced to show mostly recent work, much of it in the mother and child vein. She'd begun to rely on the motif because it was easy to like and good for sales. One reason Cassatt is so well known for these later maternal scenes is that these made up much of America's first public look at her work.

Philadelphia society, and much of New York society, followed the Cassatt family's lead and boycotted the exhibition. These were the very people who would otherwise flock to such a show, bringing money and imprimatur with them. No matter. The show was a big hit, raised good money for women's suffrage, and helped established Cassatt's reputation in her home country.

The exhibition underlined the fracture within families and between women across America, where mothers and daughters, sisters, friends, and neighbors took stands in opposition to each other. It seems ironic today that there were women so determined not to vote that they protested the possibility, organized, and were in effect politically active in hopes of defeating political engagement by women. But the Antis were powerful players in the unfolding fight, Cassatt's family passionately among them.

Cassatt, furious and hurt, lashed out. She rewrote her will, selling most of what she'd intended her nieces and nephews to inherit. This included both her own paintings and the work of friends she'd collected over decades. It was a final *screw you* to her family for not supporting women. Ellen Mary, her favorite niece, would have owned one of the greatest paintings of the nineteenth century, *The Boating Party*, now in the National Gallery of Art. Cassatt's artistic vendetta is one reason so many excellent Impressionist paintings are in American museum collections. How nice for the rest of us.

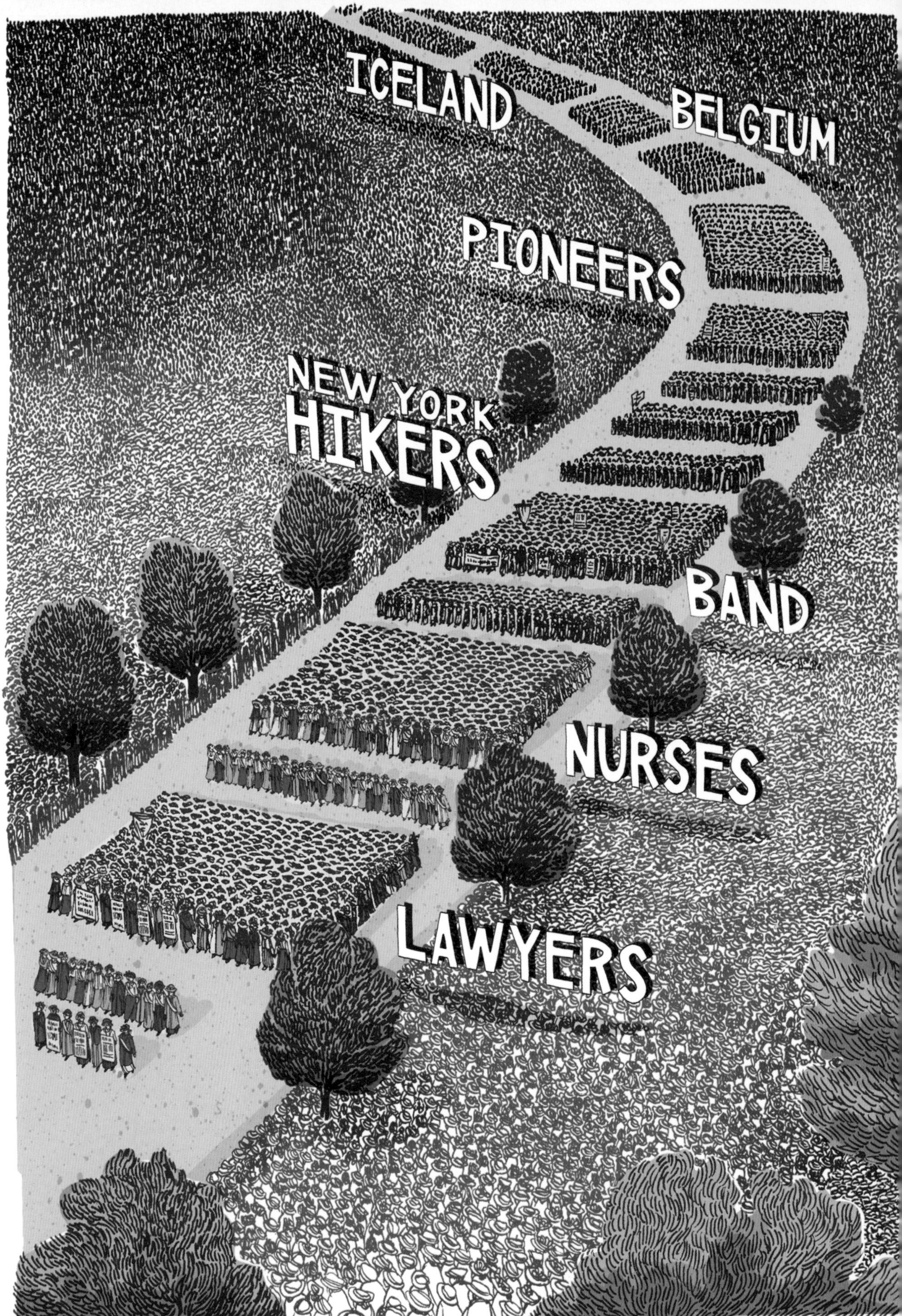
ICELAND
BELGIUM
PIONEERS
NEW YORK HIKERS
BAND
NURSES
LAWYERS

CHAPTER 7

DEEDS NOT WORDS

DEEDS NOT WORDS WAS TO BE OUR PERMANENT MOTTO.

EMMELINE PANKHURST

DAYBREAK MARCH 3, 1913, was clear and cold, with zero chance of rain or snow. The day before the inauguration of the twenty-eighth president of the United States, Woodrow Wilson, was an excellent day for a suffrage parade.

Ida B. Wells might have sat on her boardinghouse bed that morning pulling on first one pair of stockings, then another. Behind her on the coverlet may have lain the dark shapes of her heaviest skirt and coat, a thick fur muff alongside them. Bright beside those, a curving white hat covered in stars, with matching scarf and pennant. The stars signified states with full suffrage. The other side of the scarf declared in bold black letters: Illinois. Her home state. Wells no doubt

assumed she'd be alone in a sea of white women, but she wasn't afraid to stand out. Her creed, always: "One had better die fighting against injustice than to die like a dog or a rat in a trap."

The parade's instigator, Alice Paul, had made it clear that Wells and other black women ought to stay home. Their presence would only complicate matters. The suffrage message should be precise, crystal clear. Which to Paul and too many others meant white.

While a defiant Wells got dressed, Paul was probably already hunched against the cold on Pennsylvania Avenue, the broad brim of her hat tipped back to better assess the long straight shot that ran from where her buttoned boots met pavement all the way to the front door of the White House. Like a general surveying the battlefield, Paul was brooding, thoughtful, with a grim countenance to match the seriousness of her aim.

I picture her plotting over every detail in her mind, pacing slowly, with barely contained energy, like a big cat assessing its prey.

In just eight hours, upward of 8,000 women would march down Pennsylvania Avenue in orchestrated waves. Costumed, carrying signs, totally organized from tip to toe, they would broadcast their common message: "Votes for Women." There would be floats, marching bands, banners, dancing, theatrical performances, horses, and more. The setup was spectacular. At a cost of nearly $15,000 (over $382,000 in today's dollars), raised via donations spearheaded by Paul, it had better be. Paul breathed in the crisp morning air with satisfaction and allowed herself a small smile.

Paul had grown tired of talking about women's suffrage. After sixty-five years of meetings, what did suffragists have to show for themselves? Schisms and squabbles. Reunification and doldrums. And though the "founding mothers" had finally reunited their feuding organizations in 1890, what had really changed? Yes, eleven states had full suffrage, but not nearly enough. Women had a say in naming just eighty-four electors of the 483-member electoral college. Whispers drowned out by a roar. Paul was done with state-by-state ratification; it was time for a Constitutional amendment or nothing. This parade was her shot across the bow. American women were coming for what was theirs.

★ ★ ★

LIKE MANY A REVOLUTIONARY American before her, Alice Paul was a Quaker, descendent of Pennsylvania's own William Penn. So she was in some ways a born iconoclast, raised like all Quakers with the ideal of gender equity. She'd been attending suffrage meetings with her mother since shortly after her birth in 1885. Women's equality had always been as obvious to her as air and water. A fact of nature.

But Paul didn't become radicalized until she'd graduated from Swarthmore, earned her master's at Penn, and moved to England to study economics. In England, she encountered the militant suffragist—aka suffragette—a variety that had yet to reach American shores. "Deeds not words" was the motto of the British version of the movement, as embodied by its leader, Emmeline Pankhurst. Alice Paul would participate in Pankhurst's activism, then bring it home.

Let's dive into *suffragist* vs. *suffragette* waters. We may in fact be overdue, but historically here is where the terms take on significance. You might know "suffragette" from the Mary Poppins song "Sister Suffragette," or from "Suffragette City," by rock god David Bowie, both of which name check a radical movement in British history. In 1906 English women fighting for suffrage had been mockingly referred to in the *Daily Mail* as "suffragettes." As in, *Ho ho, simmer down there little ladies, you weaker sex, you mini-everything.* To which Pankhurst, leader of the Women's Social and Political Union, along with other militant ladies said, *Ha ha, why yes, we're prancing, mincing suffragettes in skirts* as they planted

bombs at St. Paul's Cathedral (and elsewhere) and threw themselves under the hooves of the king's horse. They took back the word.

Because of this association with radicalism, American women tended to prefer *suffragist* rather than *suffragette*. Counterintuitively, *suffragette* is the more radical term. Kind of like Riot Grrrl seizing power in language that sought to shame.

For her part, Paul was up for anything. Suffragette, suffragist, whatever. Deeds not words would also be her motto. Jailed seven times for her suffrage activity in Britain—a country where she wasn't even a citizen (it was the principle of the thing)—she went on hunger strike and faced the torture of being force-fed for British women. In America, she'd risk more. Prison time, forced feeding, attempted institutionalization for insanity, gunshots, public ridicule and scorn. But if she was anything, Paul was a fearless PR genius, willing to go to any lengths to give newspapers something worth writing about.

★ ★ ★

I'D GUESS IDA B. WELLS—basically dis-invited from the suffrage parade but going anyway—wished Paul would go to hell. Not that it's a competition, but as an investigative journalist and internationally known anti-lynching activist with a bull's-eye on her back, Wells was arguably the more fearless woman.

Born enslaved in Mississippi in 1862, just six months before the Emancipation Proclamation, Wells came of age in the heady years after the Civil War, nourished in the hopeful air of black freedom, which included witnessing her father and other black men vote. But such liberty did not last. Reconstruction quickly brought racist laws aimed at bringing blacks under the control of whites.

At age sixteen Wells lost both parents and her youngest brother to yellow fever. She became a teacher and raised her seven younger siblings herself. Though head of a large household, she made less than half what white teachers made. In search of better pay, Wells moved to Memphis, where she taught during the school year and attended college in the summer. A born writer, Wells never shied away from self-expression. Here she is, age twenty-four: "I will not begin at this late day by doing what my soul abhors; sugaring men, weak deceitful creatures, with flattery to retain them as escorts."

In 1889 Wells became co-owner and editor of the *Free Speech and Headlight* newspaper, where she inveighed against segregation. She high-lighted egregious examples such as the school where she taught, for which she was fired by the Memphis Board of Education. But it was in the murder of her friend Thomas Moss, owner of a popular local grocery, that Wells found her unwanted calling. Moss was dragged from a Memphis jail cell—where he was being held for the crime of defending his business from white thugs—and summarily shot along with two others. Outraged, Wells exhorted the Memphis black community in print: "There is, therefore, only one thing left to do; save our money and leave a town which will neither protect our lives and property, nor give us a fair trial in the courts, but takes us out and murders us in cold blood when accused by white persons."

An angry mob destroyed the offices of the *Free Speech and Headlight* and threatened to kill its editor. Wells bought a gun and moved to Chicago. There she got married, had four children, and conducted an international campaign to confront whites with the horror of lynching. "It is with no pleasure that I have dipped my hands in the corruption here exposed," she wrote in *Southern Horrors*, a bestseller, but "Somebody must show that the Afro-American race is more sinned against than sinning, and it seems to have fallen upon me to do so." She was thirty years old.

Frederick Douglass wrote to Wells in 1895. "I have spoken, but my word is feeble in comparison," he said, adding, "Brave woman!" Almost twenty years later, Wells was still willing to risk everything for justice.

★ ★ ★

By nine A.M. crowds already lined the Suffrage Parade route, though the official start time wasn't for six hours. By three P.M. the crowd was estimated at 500,000, many of them in D.C. for the inauguration of newly elected president Woodrow Wilson the following day. Some saw it as an amusing appetizer to the following day's main event. Some came for the spectacle of seeing women make fools of themselves in public. Some came to be inspired and to cheer on valiant women from across the country. Many came to make trouble.

As promised by the official program, a woman on horseback led the parade. Noted labor lawyer Inez Milholland—famous for her beauty—sat tall in white on a white steed, a gold crown setting off dark curls that spilled across her shoulders and down her back. She rode ahead of a banner proclaiming "Forward out of darkness, forward into light."

The *New York Times* described the effect as "one of the most impressively beautiful spectacles ever staged in this country." Behind Milholland came a horse-drawn float carrying the "Great Demand Banner" in dark caps against a white field: WE DEMAND AN AMENDMENT TO THE CONSTITUTION OF THE UNITED STATES ENFRANCHISING THE WOMEN OF THIS COUNTRY.

In other words, *We look nice; we're not playing nice.*

Following the Great Demand came seven distinct sections of marchers, including floats for each country in the world that already had national female suffrage: Australia, Finland, New Zealand, and Norway. Walking behind them were women from countries where, like the United States, women had partial suffrage. After them, women marched by profession with outfits to match, not always easy to come up with. Doctors and nurses, yes. Writers resorted to throwing ink on their clothes. Sculptor Adelaide Johnson, who would create the suffrage *Portrait Monument* from eight tons of Carrara marble (unveiled in 1921), marched with the artists. Many college-educated women marched with their alma maters, such as Vassar, Smith, Wellesley, and Bryn Mawr. Each of the forty-eight states had its own parade delegation, too (like a suffrage Olympics opening ceremony); Jeannette Rankin was among those marching for Montana, and in just three years she'd be back in D.C. as the first female member of Congress. There were women dressed as Lady

Liberty, as Columbia, as Greek maidens. Paul instructed marchers to wear the colors of the British suffragettes, green, white, and violet—their first letters standing for Give Women the Vote. But more marchers, not wanting to ally themselves with such a militant group, wore white and gold, the colors of international suffrage. There were four mounted brigades, nine marching bands, chariots, numerous floats, and more. In the *Washington Post*'s succinct subhead that day, "Floats, Bands, Skirted Calvary, and Beauties Take Part."

Not everyone was awed by the extravaganza. "The suffrage parade was too funny," wrote Eleanor Roosevelt, who watched from the sidelines. She was particularly amused by the "nice fat ladies with bare legs and feet posed in tableaux on the Treasury steps!" Those fat ladies were freezing while Eleanor giggled.

Other onlookers weren't laughing. From the beginning, men lining the route kicked, hit, and spit on women, blocking their path and nearly shutting down all forward progress. Ambulances came and went all day, and over a hundred people ended up at the local hospital. It was so contentious that according to the *Washington Post*, "doctor and driver literally had to fight their way to give succor to the injured."

The police, all men, did not come to the aid of marchers. They mostly watched in bemusement as women were spat on, struck, and groped, their costumes and banners torn, lit cigarettes thrown at them. Children in the march cried and so did some women. One policeman reportedly told women under assault, "There would be nothing like this if you women would all stay home." Much to their credit, a troop of Boy Scouts helped hold back the crowd by using walking sticks, and men from the Maryland Agriculture College used their bodies to form a human chain between the marchers and the crowd. A regiment of National Guard troops—present for the following day's inauguration—interceded to clear an intersection. Finally, order was somewhat gained by Army cavalry, staged at nearby Fort Myer at Paul's urging. The cavalry forcibly cleared a path so thousands of determined women could struggle on. The violence would prompt a Senate investigation into police culpability in failing to control the crowd and even in egging on aggression against marchers.

No one was in greater peril than the black marchers, who were segregated in the back by design.

This, I am sorry to report, must be laid squarely at the feet of Alice Paul. Well aware that Washington, D.C., is essentially a Southern city, Paul also knew how much a Constitutional amendment depended on Southern votes. So when women from Howard University, a historically black college, petitioned Paul to walk alongside their college-educated peers, Paul demurred.

For the twenty-two women of Delta Theta Sigma, the first black sorority in the American Greek system and founded at Howard less than two months before, walking in the suffrage parade would be their public coming-out party. Ida B. Wells was herself an honorary member, along with suffragist and activist Mary Church Terrell, with whom she'd help found the National Association of

Colored Women. As recently as January, Wells had co-founded the Alpha Suffrage Club of Chicago, the first African American organization dedicated to women's suffrage nationwide. These were committed suffragists, all.

But Paul was concerned that white women, especially Southern women, would balk at marching alongside black women. "As far as I can see," she told one editor, "we must have a white procession, or a Negro procession, or no procession at all."

Letters were exchanged. Paul's parent organization, the National American Women Suffrage Association (NAWSA), schooled her: All women must be permitted to march. Paul had no choice then but to "allow" Delta Theta Sigma to take part, but she did not advertise their participation in the otherwise comprehensive program of the event. And she indicated that they and other black women should march in back.

I've heard this direction by the undisputed general of the day phrased in various ways, such as, "Paul floated the idea of a discrete African American group, near the back of the parade." Or, "African Americans were encouraged to march in a segregated group near the end of the lineup." *Floated. Encouraged.* It couldn't have been so passive as that, and Ida B. Wells knew it. "If the Illinois women do not take a stand now in this great democratic parade then the colored women are lost. . . .

I shall not march at all unless I can march under the Illinois banner," she informed her delegation. But Illinois white women did not take a united stand in defense of black women. The Illinois contingent told Wells to go to the back of the lineup. She refused, and when her state was well underway in the parade, Wells stepped out of the crowd and marched with them alongside her white friends Virginia Brooks and Bell Squire.

On March 5 Chicago's *Daily Tribune* published a triumphant picture of Wells and her supporters en route. At least three other states—Delaware, Michigan, and New York—had not given in to segregation. Not nearly enough.

To Alice Paul, the Great Suffrage Parade of 1913 was an overwhelming success. Never had women's suffrage received so much sympathetic national press. If it took women taking some beatings and harsh words, so be it.

But the parade illuminated yet again the racism at the heart of white suffragism. Such fixation on voting rights solely for white women would bear fruit in the limitations of the Nineteenth Amendment itself. "A white woman has only one handicap to overcome," wrote marcher Mary Church Terrell, "that of sex. I have two—both sex and race." For women of color, the fight for equal voting rights would still carry on for decades.

CHAPTER

8

EARLY ARRIVAL:
JEANNETTE RANKIN

Are not our menfolk inconsistent? They fear lest women in politics should act like men — and now that we have a woman in Congress they demand that she act like a man!

EDITH AYERS, ISMAY, MONTANA, 1917

Carrie Chapman Catt

IN LATE MARCH 1917, Carrie Chapman Catt, head of the National American Woman Suffrage Association, met Jeannette Rankin at NAWSA's Manhattan headquarters. Rankin was pit-stopping briefly in New York on her way to Washington, and came by to pay respects at America's largest suffrage organization.

You might expect Catt would be pleased to see a woman take her seat in Congress before American women even had the right to vote nationally. After all, the victory of Republican Jeannette Rankin of Montana was the very embodiment of Catt's "Winning Plan" of securing votes for women state by state, while simultaneously pushing for a Constitutional amendment. But Catt was disappointed that the first woman to hold national office was not from New York, Boston, Philadelphia—someplace, in other words, that *mattered*—but from a sparsely populated Western state. What power was there in that?

Catt further feared Rankin's other short-comings could prove terminal to women's hopes nationwide. Rankin wasn't a lawyer, much less an intellectual. Not a mother, not even married. Not rich or well-connected. Not in any way an ideal representative of American womanhood. In other words, not much help to the cause that Catt could see.

On the contrary, Rankin might easily prove a disaster. For one thing, she was a Republican and Catt had thrown NAWSA behind Democratic president Woodrow Wilson. If suffragists hoped to ever see a Constitutional amendment, they needed the president on their side. Catt hoped to convince Rankin to support Wilson, even if he declared war.

Rankin had run on a pacifist platform, true, but even pacifists had to be pragmatic if they wanted to win. She must understand that, more than representing an inconsequential state, she now represented every woman in America. Rankin could make or break them all.

One of the most politically powerful women in America, Catt expected Rankin to fall in line under her leadership of NAWSA. But Rankin toed nobody's line but her own.

★ ★ ★

THIRTY-SIX-YEAR-OLD Jeannette Rankin had grown up on her family's Grant Creek Ranch six miles outside Missoula and could ride, rope, and shoot as well as she could sew, bake a pie, speak persuasively, and shatter stereotypes. She was in New York at the insistence of her brilliant campaign manager (her only brother, Wellington), to make a glad-handing stop on the way to take her seat in Washington, D.C.. Everyone was watching and fawning, for the most part. Even the *New York Times* was now reporting seriously on her suffrage work, while before her election it had run sarcastic editorials about her "wealth of red hair" and how her election might improve the House "aesthetically."

Her hair was not red, and Rankin was not amused. That her win had been a drubbing came as a great shock to everyone but her.

Counter to Carrie Catt's take on her, Rankin was neither uneducated nor unworldly. She had received a degree in biology from the University of Montana in 1902 and taken classes at the New York School of Philanthropy. She'd lived in Massachusetts,

California, Washington State, New York, and D.C. And she was as committed to suffrage as anyone. After Montana women won the vote in 1914, Rankin worked as a field secretary for NAWSA, then as a lobbyist in Washington, D.C. With all that, and with the newly enfranchised women of Montana at her back, in November 1916 she bested her older Democratic opponent, Colonel E. Jacob Crull, by over seven thousand votes.

"I'm heartbroken," Crull purportedly proclaimed, before killing himself on the steps of a funeral home the following spring.

Yes, losing to a woman was that bad. Newspapers blamed Rankin for his death.

★ ★ ★

REGARDLESS, RANKIN'S SWEARING IN on April 2, 1917, was a festive affair, complete with parade, bunting, speeches. Her office—the press noted with glee that it was across the hall from that of a "bachelor" representative—was filled with congratulatory flowers. Choosing a bunch in approximate suffrage colors of yellow and violet, Rankin carried them to the House floor, where she hesitated, unsure which desk was hers. Men got to their feet and cheered. Someone showed Rankin to her seat. When her name was called to be sworn in, the room erupted again. Rankin grinned, waved, sat down, then rose to acknowledge further applause before it finally subsided.

It was a glorious day, a kind of heaven.

It did not last.

That evening President Wilson delivered his address to a joint session of Congress, calling for war with Germany after their resumption of unrestricted submarine combat. America's neutrality had been attacked and "the world must be made safe for democracy," Wilson declared. (Though America's democracy did not yet include women.)

That fast, Jeannette Rankin was in hell.

Two days later the Senate approved the declaration, with just six dissenting votes. Now it went to the House. Catt insisted it was Rankin's womanly duty to support the nation in war. Otherwise women looked weak, unable to seize the hardest tasks of leadership, and even traitorous. Wellington assured his sister that if she voted against, her political career was over. He urged her to cast a "man's vote" for war. Rankin, wrote influential suffragist and socialite Harriet Laidlaw, underwent "one of the most terrible mental struggles any woman ever had."

Debate in the House began on April 5 and continued into early morning of April 6. Finally, at three A.M., the roll was called. Rankin was set to cast the first legislative vote by a woman in American history. But at the sound of her name, she did not answer.

When roll was called a second time, she did respond, but not by recognized protocol with a simple "aye" or "nay." Instead Rankin rose slowly to her feet and said, "I want to stand by my country, but I cannot vote for war." The clerk asked whether that meant she was voting against the declaration. She was.

"Think what you've done," Wellington lamented as they walked back in the dark to her new apartment on California Street.

Forty-nine other members of Congress voted against the war, along with six senators, but all attention was on Rankin. The *Times* wrote that she'd been "overcome by her ordeal" and many newspapers reported that she'd sobbed, swooned, even fainted. None of which was true. Legendary New York Congressman Fiorello La Guardia said that he'd not seen Rankin crying, but then he'd had a hard time focusing through his own tears.

Fellow suffragists were less supportive. After Rankin's No vote, Catt wrote a friend, "Our Congress Lady is a sure enough joker. Whatever she has done or will do is wrong to somebody, and every time she answers a roll call she loses us a million votes."

The naysayers were right on one score. Rankin was not reelected. But on the larger question, history suggests Rankin was not unwise since World War I—the "war to end war"—led to the even greater devastation of World War II. As fate would have it, Rankin returned to Congress in 1941, and that same year, the day after the attack on Pearl Harbor, she cast the only "nay" vote against authorizing war with Japan. She was not reelected.

★ ★ ★

FOR HER RESILIENCE and persistence and courage, she was commemorated in bronze, instead. In 1985 a statue of Rankin was installed in the Capitol in Washington. By chance, the artist is my cousin. But the commission itself seemed destined. The *New York Times* wrote of the unveiling, "The Rankin statue was crafted by Terry Mimnaugh, a Montana artist who bears a striking resemblance to Miss Rankin in

JEANNETTE
RANKIN

her young years." A teenager then, I was in awe of both women. And as when I learned of artist Alice Cooper sculpting Sacajawea, I felt inspired by the symmetry of witnessing one generation of talented women in the West honoring another.

When Rankin's heroic bronze was dedicated in Washington, she was the only woman associated with suffrage in sight. The *Portrait Monument* depicting Lucretia Mott, Elizabeth Cady Stanton, and Susan B. Anthony still rested down below in the Capitol Crypt, where it had languished for over fifty years. To my knowledge, there is no sculpture in the Capitol dedicated to Carrie Chapman Catt.

CHAPTER 9

LAW BREAKING TO LAW MAKING

How shall we answer the challenge, gentlemen? How shall we explain to them the meaning of democracy if the same Congress that voted to make the world safe for democracy refuses to give this small measure of democracy to the women of our country?

JEANNETTE RANKIN, 1918
U.S. HOUSE OF REPRESENTATIVES

ON THE MORNING OF Woodrow Wilson's 1913 inauguration, Harriot Stanton Blatch (remember her, daughter of Elizabeth Cady Stanton?), shot him a telegram (copied to major newspapers): "As you ride today in comfort and safety to the Capitol to be inaugurated as President of the people of the United States, we beg that you will not be unmindful that yesterday the Government which is supposed to exist for the good of all, left women while passing in peaceful procession in the demand for political freedom at the mercy of a howling mob on the very streets which are being at this moment efficiently officered for the protection of men."

Said more succinctly by another marcher: the police would have "taken better care of a drove of pigs." The U.S. Senate opened an investigation. Locally, the chief of police

was fired. Nationally, a women's fringe issue suddenly seized center stage.

Wilson, for his part, did nothing.

Less than a year after the Suffrage Parade, history repeated itself and women's suffrage again split into rival camps. The larger, more conservative National American Woman Suffrage Association (NAWSA) focused its energy on a state-by-state solution. Alice Paul's smaller, increasingly militant National Women's Party (NWP) insisted on an amendment to the Constitution, *or else*.

By 1916, NAWSA was headed by Carrie Chapman Catt, veteran of the suffrage wars. You've met her already (see Jeannette Rankin) and more on her to come, but for now suffice to say that Catt and Paul were like generals in competing armies, with a common enemy. Maybe like Britain and Russia in World War II:

One wore a proper stiff upper lip and stayed the course, the other preferred the Bolshevik approach, rebellious and revolutionary.

Despite valiant efforts on the ground by NAWSA, just two states—Nevada and Montana—granted women's suffrage between 1914 and 1916, while Nebraska, Missouri, Ohio, and North and South Dakota voted it down. This only confirmed Paul's determination to push for a federal amendment. In 1916 her NWP crisscrossed America on a thirty-eight-day train tour to speak out for a suffrage amendment. Star of the "Suffrage Special" was none other than Inez Milholland, as riveting onstage as she'd been in D.C. astride that white horse.

But so much travel and public speaking took its toll. Milholland collapsed in Los Angeles on the tour, much sicker than anyone had realized. As she lay dying, Wilson was elected to a second term. Milholland's last words, according to her sister, Vida, were, "President Wilson, how long must this go on—no liberty?"

In memory of Milholland's ultimate sacrifice, in early January 1917, Paul and three hundred fellow suffragists met with newly reelected President Wilson at the White House, asking him to honor the death of a courageous young woman by supporting her fight for a federal amendment. Wilson had expected some ceremonial handover of vague resolutions tied up in a pretty package, not scores of serious women outright asking for the vote. I imagine him first jolly and welcoming—*Well hello ladies, gosh there's ever so many of you and don't you all look so nice in white, very seasonable, ha ha*—then growing chilly. Surprised by their temerity in so baldly broaching politics, Wilson coldly refused. And old college prof that he was, he couldn't resist scolding the assembled women with a patronizing lecture on the nature of party politics. He departed as soon as he was finished lecturing, leaving hundreds of women in stunned silence.

★ ★ ★

WILSON HAD NO IDEA what fury he'd unleashed. Back at NWP's new headquarters on Lafayette Square, directly across Pennsylvania Avenue from the White House, Stanton Blatch seethed. "We can't organize bigger processions. We can't, women, do anything more in that line. We have got to take a new departure. We have got to keep the question before him all the time. We have got to begin and begin immediately," she said, lighting a new, fierce fire under her troops. Alice Paul was all in. The very next morning twelve women left NWP headquarters to take up positions outside the White House, six at each main gate. They dressed alike: long dark coats (some with fur trim at hem and sleeves), sensible low-heeled button-up boots, hats, gloves, sashes, and standards (in suffrage colors of gold, white, and violet). They were soldiers ready for battle.

Lest their matching outfits and tall standards weren't arresting enough, two of the women carried banners with dark lettering on a pale background. One read: "Mr. President What Will You Do for Woman Suffrage?" The other quoted Inez Milholland's dying words: "Mr. President How Long Must Women Wait for Liberty?"

These were the Silent Sentinels, gathered in voiceless rebuke. It was the first time in

American history anyone had thought to picket the White House.

Wilson's first encounter with the women came around eleven A.M. that first day. He was riding in the backseat of his chauffeured car, returning from a round of golf; maybe he was engrossed in reading about himself in the newspaper, maybe he saw them out of the corner of his eye and made a concerted effort not to turn his head. Whatever the reason, he did not look, an unforgivable snub of the highest order. His eldest daughter, Margaret, also in the backseat (and pro-women's suffrage) giddily waved.

The following day was freezing. Wilson sent a message to the picketers offering warm drinks. The women declined, shortened their shifts, and again stayed past dusk. They intended to protest until Wilson's second

inauguration (two months away), unless he supported a federal amendment first.

While the White House initially shrugged, editorial page writers and others found the protest unfathomable and enraging. One *New York Times* headline read: "Silent, Silly, and Offensive." Only women, the *Times* despaired, could concoct such a scheme "compounded of pettiness and monstrosity." But all that winter, day after day, the sentinels stood on.

Finally, March 4, the day intended to be their last, dawned wet and cold. As a grand finale, they'd planned a procession of one thousand picketers to present their resolution for women's suffrage to the president, and thus end this standoff. They marched confidently out to the gates, only to find them deliberately locked. Wilson would have the last word by denying them theirs. Silently, en masse, dripping and freezing in slickers and rain hats, they circled the White House, led by Vida Milholland, sister of their departed saint.

It was unintentional PR gold, just the kind of grand display the NWP did best. Journalists wrote of the event in biblical terms, a circling of Jericho by the Israelites. (Wherein Joshua and his army marched three times around the ancient city blowing horns and, as the old spiritual goes, "the walls come tumbling down.")

Suddenly the White House gates opened, but not to allow envoys from the protest in. Instead, Wilson's limousine, with the president snug and dry inside, passed out of the White House yard, the gates swinging closed behind him. Again, he did not glance sideways.

The sentinels vowed then to keep up their vigil for as long as it took.

Again, war intervened. On April 6, 1917, America declared war on Germany and entered World War I. Woodrow Wilson's campaign promise—to keep the United States out of the European theater (his other promise was "America first," but that's another story)— was now broken. The suffragists, sensing weakness, doubled down. They maintained their posts at the White House gates all that spring.

Their enemies grew increasingly incensed. Crowds declared them unpatriotic. There was heckling, spitting, kicking. Men routinely destroyed the sentinels' banners.

The women stood their ground.

The first generation of suffragists shelved their fight during the Civil War, just as the suffragettes in Britain were shelving theirs at that very moment across the Atlantic. But Alice

Paul had written her dissertation on the history of suffrage, and she'd long believed that relinquishing their push during the Civil War prolonged the suffrage fight by at least seventy years. A men's war was no reason for women to relinquish theirs, she said.

★ ★ ★

THAT SUMMER, SENTINEL banners got saltier. In June, after a U.S. envoy to Russia proclaimed America a place of "universal, equal, direct, and secret suffrage," the NWP cooked up a banner to greet the Russian envoys on their return visit. The text was far too long for Russians to read when driving by on their way to the White House but can be summarized in two of the lines: "We, the women of America, tell you that America is not democracy. Twenty million American women are denied the right to vote."

Treason! Some onlookers were so enraged they brandished knives at women holding the offensive signs. The banners were sliced to ribbons.

The next day an identical banner went up. (The NWP had confirmed with lawyers that the text was neither libelous nor treasonous.)

The abuse continued until, finally, on the third day, arrests occurred. But not of the men assaulting peaceful protesters. Oh no. Just the sentinels. They were charged with—wait for it—obstructing the sidewalk; Wilson was too savvy to infringe directly on their First Amendment right to free speech.

The next six months saw the arrest of some five hundred women, with around one hundred and fifty actually going to jail. Many were

mothers, even grandmothers. Sisters were sometimes jailed together, as well as mothers and their daughters, and mothers of young men fighting in Europe at that very moment for freedom and democracy. Some were wives and daughters of prominent men and some of those were friends of Wilson. Sentinel Alison Hopkins had been to dinner with the Wilsons not long before her jail sentence. Her furious husband upbraided Wilson, asking how he'd like it if it was the president's wife, Edith Wilson, bedding down "next to prostitutes."

Finally, the president blinked.

The arrests of wives and daughters of friends and supporters was not a good look.

Wilson, acting swiftly to save face, began handing out pardons. He did not anticipate that nearly everyone released would go straight back to protesting. Wilson could take his pardon and shove it.

"Obstructing traffic" became a cat-and-mouse game of imprisonment and release, imprisonment, release. D.C. judges and the wardens of D.C.'s District Jail were apoplectic. The visuals were terrible.

They got worse.

On July 4, eleven women marched on the White House carrying banners that, like the Declaration of Rights and Sentiments, paraphrased the Declaration of Independence: "Governments derive their just powers from the consent of the governed." They were arrested almost immediately. How dare they bring up liberty on Independence Day? Newspapers took note.

On July 14—Bastille Day in France, celebrating the day revolutionaries stormed a Paris prison and unleashed the French Revolution—sixteen be-sashed women in long skirts and wide-brimmed hats marched on the White House. This coterie was, by chance, particularly well connected to men of note, including journalists, ambassadors, and politicians. One banner proclaimed the ideals of the French Revolution: "Liberty, Equality, Fraternity, July 14, 1789." (Maybe the fraternity part was a little tongue in cheek, but regardless, the point was made: Liberty, or else.)

The Francophiles were, of course, arrested. All routine, except this time the judge upped the punishment: Pay the fine or go to the workhouse for sixty days (previously the sentences had been more like three days). He assumed the women would pay rather than commit to real jail time. But paying fines was an admission of guilt. These suffragists were pleading not guilty.

And so the prison population at the Occoquan Women's Workhouse in Virginia (the main outpost for imprisoned suffragists) ballooned.

The tide of public opinion was turning. Pressure mounted. Wilson pardoned the offenders after just three days (among them Alison Hopkins).

As *thanks*, on August 14, sentinels carried their most strident banner yet: "KAISER WILSON, Have you forgotten your sympathy with the poor Germans because they were not self-governed. 20,000,000 American women are not self-governed. . . ."

Violence against the sentinels intensified. Women were kicked, pushed, battered, and dragged; banners destroyed; a shot fired into NWP national headquarters. More arrests were made. The women demanded political

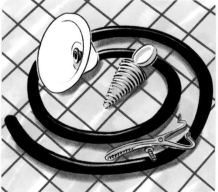

prisoner status—a canny card from the British suffragette playbook—to which Wilson countered with a succinct "Never."

Fine. Paul was sick of the cat-mouse game already. It was time to pull out the biggest gun in the suffragette arsenal: the hunger strike. Paul volunteered to go first. Others quickly followed. A doctor from St. Elizabeths Insane Asylum was called in to have Paul forcibly committed, a popular strategy for dealing with unruly women since the dawn of the patriarchy, but alas, he found her sane. He did recommend force-feeding, though, which the prison authorities took up with gusto.

Akin to waterboarding, force-feeding is "a form of torture" according to the ACLU, and that was assuredly how it was used. Women choked up vomit and blood three times a day. At Occoquan, where most of them were stowed, women were pushed down stairs, hurled against metal bed frames, locked into "punishment cells" in total darkness. One particularly awful "Night of Terror" saw one NWP leader, Lucy Burns, calling out to other women in pitch blackness to see if any were seriously injured, causing guards to handcuff her to a cell door with her arms above her head like

a cartoon prisoner in the *New Yorker*. All of this was, remember, for a charge of "obstructing traffic" on a sidewalk.

When NWP lawyers filed a writ of habeas corpus—basically demanding that the women physically be seen in court—because they had been illegally transferred out of the district, the state countered that they'd sent only "able-bodied prisoners" to Occoquan for humanitarian reasons, a work house after all rather than a "real" prison. At this, NWP lawyers had seventy-three-year-old Mary Nolan, weak from hunger and mistreatment, rise unsteadily to her feet. Within the week, they all had their freedom.

That no one died from hunger strikes was a blessing, both for the women and for the Wilson administration. In all, thirty women refused to eat and not one had broken down, despite torture and temptation (fried chicken, warm milk, buttered toast). They and other imprisoned sentinels were living martyrs to the cause, celebrated throughout the movement. One of those imprisoned was Mary Cassatt's old friend Louisine Havemeyer, a rich, well-connected grandmother who went to jail for burning Woodrow Wilson in effigy outside the White House. She knew she'd be arrested, that was practically the whole point. She'd packed a small bag with warm clothes and disinfectant. Marching along the sidewalk with a standard and, presumably, matches, she said she'd felt "as placid and calm as if I were going out to play croquet on a summer afternoon."

Havemeyer could have afforded the most precious jewels, but after her release she, like all the jailed sentinels, received a coveted gift from the NWP. In a move inspired by British suffragette pins, each woman was given a silver brooch replica of a jail cell door, complete with bars, an opening for food to be passed through, and a tiny chain across it that ended in a heart-shaped lock. This was a precious token for the women who'd gone to jail in

support of suffrage, something no money could buy.

★ ★ ★

In January 1918, after many months of protest, Woodrow Wilson at last declared his support for the Susan B. Anthony amendment. Protests no doubt helped persuade him, but so did the work of Carrie Chapman Catt's NAWSA efforts state by state. Enough Democratic states had now ratified women's suffrage that support for a Constitutional amendment was deemed safe for the national party to get behind. Even so, Wilson's backing was tepid, even cool. His statement to leaders of the Democratic Party included the caveat that "any member of Congress opposed to woman suffrage for

any reason ought not to vote other than his conviction." Hardly a ringing endorsement.

It took months of further protest, glad-handing, threats, speeches, and multiple votes, and still the amendment resolution failed to pass both houses. Then, on November 11, 1918, World War I ended. The world had been made safe for democracy. The following spring, on June 4, 1919, the Susan B. Anthony amendment was at last passed by both houses of the United States legislature. It was a start. But now it was up to states—three-fourths of them required—to vote in favor of ratification before the Nineteenth Amendment could become national law.

CHAPTER 10

WAR OF THE ROSES

I am here representing the mothers who are at home rocking the cradle, and not representing the low-neck and high-skirt variety who know not what it is to go down in the shade of the valley and bring forth children. Motherhood has no appeal for them.

HERSCHEL CANDLER, TENNESSEE SENATE, 1920

A MOTHER'S ADVICE IS ALWAYS SAFEST FOR A BOY TO FOLLOW.

HARRY BURN, TENNESSEE HOUSE OF REPRESENTATIVES, 1920

WEDNESDAY, AUGUST 18, 1920, dawned piercingly clear. Nashville's limestone statehouse shone in the early sun like a beacon up on Capitol Hill. The day felt scrubbed clean. Crowds of women and men, entire families, children and old people included, made their eager way uphill and then, without complaint, further up the seventy-two statehouse steps. The first of them quickly filled the gallery overlooking the floor of the Tennessee House of Representatives. Many more were left standing along hallways or on balconies or covered porticoes, or perched on steps or low walls, or sat right down on the grassy lawns sloping back toward town. It would have felt festive, a great civic celebration, if a current of tension

hadn't buzzed through the crowd like a live wire ready to catch fire and explode.

By nine it was getting hot. By ten the air was heavy with humidity. Roses wilted, soft petals shrinking into tight fists where they were pinned above the heart on ladies' dresses and along men's lapels. Josephine Pearson, fifty-one years old, gray-haired, and sturdy, stood at the top of the statehouse steps and scanned the crowd. Satisfied that she saw more red and pink roses than yellow, she smiled, turned and strode inside. One of the best seats in the gallery—where she could take in the whole floor of the legislature at a glance—was being held for her. Pearson was, by now, one of the most famous women in Tennessee.

By day's end she also expected to be the most celebrated.

Inside the cool stone interior of the statehouse she paused and gave thanks. To God, and to the memory of her blessed mother. On her deathbed, Amanda Pearson had grasped Josephine's hand with surprising strength, "Daughter, when I'm gone—if the Susan B. Anthony amendment issue reaches Tennessee—promise me, you will take up the opposition, in My Memory!" Josephine had promised. Now here she was, president of the Tennessee State Association Opposed to Woman Suffrage and head of the Tennessee division of the Southern Women's League for the Rejection of the Susan B. Anthony Amendment, leading the Antis to victory. Pearson might have wept, but she was too damned happy.

A young man bumped her shoulder as he rushed past and she stumbled. "Pardon, ma'am," he said, stopping to take her arm. He was well brought up. Pearson approved. "I was told Mr. Burn needs this right away." He held up a thick envelope and Pearson stood aside, making a gesture for him to carry on. "By all means," she said. She'd seen young representative Harry Burn when he arrived, looking rumpled and undone, hair barely combed, eyes bloodshot and baggy, but a dewy red rose pinned just above the pocket of his suit jacket. He was one of theirs.

On Tuesday, the Antis had run a boldfaced ad in the morning paper, exhorting those who would defeat the Susan B. Anthony amendment to "Wear a red or pink rose. Show your loyalty to the people of your own land. In the name of millions of Southern women we appeal to the unquestioned chivalry of the South." Pearson touched the trio of crimson rosebuds resting against her considerable bosom.

Countering the Antis, "Suffs" wore yellow roses and promoted suffrage colors wherever they could in boutonnieres, bunting, dresses, and hats. They had filled the chamber with enough white and yellow in support of suffrage that there was even a sunflower mounted above the Speaker's chair.

On the floor of the legislature, twenty-eight-year-old Speaker of the House Seth Walker strode from desk to desk, shaking hands and slapping men on the back. Bucking them up. He'd once leaned Suff, but when it came to brass tacks—that is, the federal government shoving a Constitutional amendment down the throats of Southern men—he turned Anti for good. He'd not forgotten how the Fourteenth and Fifteenth Amendments had been imposed on the South during Reconstruction. Such federalism would never again happen on his watch. States' rights and Southern sovereignty forever! Walker's high, smooth forehead was shiny with sweat. Not from nervousness, but from anticipation. Seth Walker saw himself as the Anti hero of the House. He straightened his tie and adjusted his white cuffs. He was ready.

Joe Hanover glanced up to see Walker glad-handing farmers-turned-legislators from every corner of the state. Hanover was thumbing through his list of promised pro-ratification voters, a yellow rose tucked into the buttonhole of his jacket. Though a Democrat like Walker, Hanover was Suff all the way and floor leader of the pro-ratification forces.

A Jewish immigrant from Poland who'd come to Tennessee at age eleven, he understood better than most the shining promise of American democracy. He'd left his job as district attorney and rejoined the legislature specifically to work for ratification of the Nineteenth Amendment. So far his tireless toil had mostly earned him epithets, Kike and Bolshevik chief among them, but also threats. The governor had recently assigned him a bodyguard.

Hanover's persuasive technique was very different from Walker's. That weekend a long-time ally told him, "Sorry, Joe, but I'm going to have to leave you suffrage boys. The Antis just paid me three hundred dollars." Hanover hadn't flinched. "Well, you're a pretty cheap vote," he'd said, keeping his nose down in the Sunday paper, "I hear they're paying the others a thousand." Enraged at Anti perfidy, the man switched his vote back and said this time he wouldn't budge. Bribes were among the easiest Anti tactics for Hanover to counter. Harder was keeping his men out of the Jack Daniel's room at the Hermitage Hotel, where Anti whiskey flowed like water despite Prohibition. Tougher still were phone calls from soft-voiced ladies late at night, claiming to be Suffs and inviting men to their rooms, where photographers no doubt waited to capture compromising shots. Hanover grinned at the idea, then frowned. He'd come to the end of his list. There weren't enough votes.

Republican Harry Burn, youngest member of the House at age twenty-two, was slumped at his desk when an even younger legislative page slipped around Walker and thrust an envelope his way. It wasn't until Burn

recognized his mother's handwriting that he understood he should take it. Burn rubbed his eyes—he'd slept badly—and opened it without much thinking. He counted seven pages from his widowed mother back in tiny Niota. They were from a small town in a conservative district, where most folks believed women had all the say they needed via their husbands and fathers. His constituents generally still agreed with what Tennessee's former governor had said a dozen years ago now: "Let the women pray and the men vote." Burn knew that's what the Louisiana and Nashville Railroad believed. The railroad was a family business of a sort. He was an agent, and his father had been stationmaster of the Niota train depot for some thirty years. Burn sighed. He knew what was expected of him.

He turned to his mom's letter (her name was Febb Ensminger Burn, for the record), hoping to lose himself in home while the world roiled around him. News of family, weather, nice everyday things. Burn smoothed the first sheet and started reading.

Dear Son: Hurrah and vote for suffrage and don't keep them in doubt. I noticed Chandler's speech, it was very bitter. I've been waiting to see how you stood but have not seen anything yet. Don't forget to be a good boy and help Mrs. Catt....

His mother had misspelled Senator Candler's name, but she'd nailed the man himself. Burn glanced around, though no one was paying attention to the youngest junior rep from Niota, and quickly stuffed the letter into his jacket pocket, beneath the red corsage on his chest.

★ ★ ★

YOU KNOW THAT HEMINGWAY line in *The Sun Also Rises*—which takes place right around these same years—where a character says he went bankrupt "Two ways. Gradually and then suddenly"? That's how it was with women's suffrage: slow, incremental gains (alongside many losses) and then suddenly, bam.

When the so-called Susan B. Anthony amendment had finally passed both houses of the United States Congress on June 4, 1919, the battle was of course far from done, since amendments to the Constitution require ratification by a three-fourths majority of states. In 1920 America had forty-eight states (Alaska and Hawaii were still territories), which meant thirty-six of them needed to vote to ratify the Nineteenth Amendment if it was

to become part of the U.S. Constitution. That's a lot of men up for giving women more power. And yet things went pretty smoothly for the Suffs early on.

Wisconsin became the first state to vote for ratification, on June 10, 1919. By the summer of 1920, thirty-five states had voted yes, while eight voted it down, which meant ratification required just one more "yes" to pass. Awesome, but not so fast. Vermont, Connecticut, and Florida refused to call special sessions before the 1920 presidential election in November. That left North Carolina—with pretty much no hope of ratification—and Tennessee—iffy, but still hope—where both governors had called special sessions. If the Nineteenth Amendment wasn't ratified soon, not only would most women not be able to vote in the 1920 election, but momentum would be lost and a new president and Congress could portend disaster. Delay might easily mean the death of the Susan B. Anthony amendment forever.

It came down to Tennessee. By mid-July 1920, pro- and anti-ratification forces (Suffs and Antis) had descended on Nashville, where the lobbying, grandstanding, bribery, and dirty tricks came thick and fast. Surprisingly, ratification passed in the Tennessee Senate by a margin of twenty-five to four on Friday, August 13. But the rhetoric was ugly. Senator H. M. Candler, for example, declared that women's suffrage would mean that "Tennessee would have negroes down here to represent her in the legislature," then said it would lead to black men marrying white women, and rounded it off with an extended personal attack on Suff leader Carrie Chapman Catt.

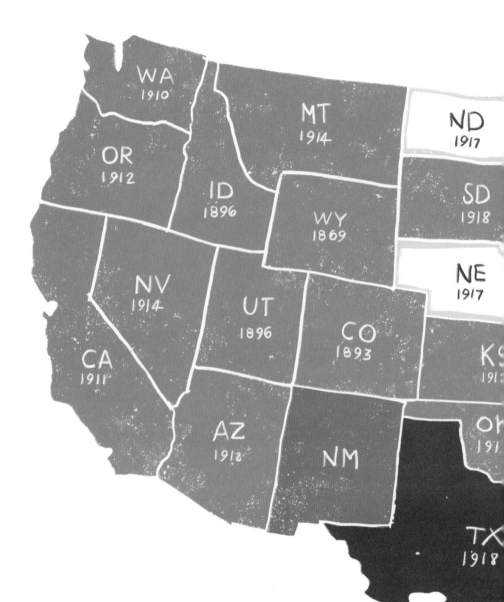

WA
1910

MT
1914

ND
1917

OR
1912

ID
1896

SD
1918

WY
1869

NE
1917

NV
1914

UT
1896

CO
1893

KS
1912

CA
1911

AZ
1912

NM

OK
191

TX
1918

FULL
SUFFRAGE

PRIMARY
SUFFRAGE

PRESIDENTIAL
SUFFRAGE

MUNICIPAL
SUFFRAGE

MN

WI

MI
1918

IA

IL
1913

IN

MO

KY

AR
1917

TN

MS

AL

GA

SC

NC

LA

FL

OH
1917

WV

VA

PA

MD

NJ

DE

NY
1917

VT

NH

MA

CT

RI
1917

ME

PRESIDENTIAL & MUNICIPAL SUFFRAGE

MUNICIPAL SUFFRAGE IN CHARTER CITIES

SCHOOL BOND or TAX

NO SUFFRAGE

Whatever. As Catt wrote hopefully from Nashville, "We are one half of one state away from victory."

Ratification now went to the House, where votes pro and anti were neck and neck. But by Monday night Seth Walker crowed to reporters, "We've got 'em whipped to a frazzle. We have ratification beaten, that is all there is to it."

Many of those camped out in Memphis, like Anti powerhouse Josephine Pearson, were Tennessee natives, though not all Tennessee women were against suffrage by a long shot. Seated not far from Pearson in the gallery was fellow native daughter Sue Shelton White, a yellow rose fixed alongside the prison-door pin she always wore. White was the only Tennessee woman ever jailed for suffrage. She'd been a Silent Sentinel, one of those sentenced to Occoquan Workhouse. Alice Paul's general on the ground in Nashville, White led the radical suffrage charge. Though partly the result of lack of funds, having White stand in for Paul proved wise. No one could accuse White of carpetbagging. She was as homegrown a fighter as any Tennessee Volunteer.

White sat a little taller on the hard gallery chair and slowly fanned herself with the score-card she had on hand to tally votes as they were called. This waiting game was tougher than any hunger strike.

★ ★ ★

CARRIE CHAPMAN CATT KNEW about waiting. In her room at the Hermitage Hotel, where she'd been living for over a month, Catt sat at an open window, eyes locked on the statehouse. As head of NAWSA, the larger, more subtle wing of the women's suffrage fight, Catt had corresponded with Wilson for years, privately winning him with honey while Paul bludgeoned him in public. But Catt was no less committed or tenacious. A suffrage warrior for more than three decades, she'd been one of Aunt Susan's Girls in Anthony's intimate circle. As a well-known public figure in the fight for women's rights, and a Yankee, it was just good politics for her to stay out of sight.

As a result, Catt might not have seen the large ad by the Antis in the *Tennessean* that morning, titled "The Truth About the Negro Problem" and warning of a RACE WAR in all caps. But had she seen it, she likely wouldn't have been shocked. Catt had made her own comments about opposing interracial marriage in hopes of winning Southern hearts. White suffragists were yet again unable to resist wielding race as a weapon in their voting fight.

Just after ten thirty A.M., Seth Walker called the House to order. Ninety-six of ninety-nine representatives were in attendance. One of the missing was a pro-suffrage legislator who'd raced back home to be with his gravely ill wife.

"The hour has come," Walker proclaimed. "The battle has been fought and it is won." And with that, he moved to table the vote.

Josephine Pearson cheered and grabbed the nearest Anti for a bear hug. "No!" shouted Susan White. Suff women roared in anger and frustration, while Antis cheered.

Tabling meant there would be no vote. It could be put off and off and off. For many legislators on both sides this was ideal. There could be little political fallout to simply asking for more time. Suffrage supporters feared the worst.

The clerk commenced roll call. The first men said "no" and Suffs cheered. Then the B names mostly went "aye." Along with them, Harry Burn voted for tabling. On it went, back and forth. Hanover voted against. Walker waded among the delegates, putting his arm over shoulders, urging men to vote with him. Only one resisted his pressure, a redheaded farmer named Banks Turner. He was a political ally of the Suff governor, but he'd voted Anti with Walker on previous votes. Yet now Turner surprised Walker, and everyone, by voting against tabling. That sealed it. The ballot was tied forty-eight to forty-eight. The motion was not carried.

Cheers and boos from the gallery. Antis were furious. Suffs celebrated, while praying this meant Turner was secretly Suff.

His first gambit having failed, Walker called for an immediate vote on ratification, believing he still had the votes to signal the end of the Nineteenth Amendment for good.

Roll was called again, this time to decide everything. Again the votes went one way, then the next. In the gallery, women hunched over scorecards ticking boxes next to names. A few Suffs could not stop the tears.

However, this time when the clerk said his name, young Harry Burn answered with a soft, swift "Aye." The clerk was on to other names before the change registered. Women in the gallery jumped to their feet. Burn's sudden shift made it a tie. But to win they still needed one more Anti to vote Suff. Turner had seemed

with them during the tabling vote; maybe there was hope.

Walker glared at turncoat Harry Burn, who did not meet his gaze, then crossed the floor to Banks Turner. Maybe he'd voted not to table because he was a tough son of a bitch who wanted the thing done right: outright defeat. Walker leaned down and whispered in Turner's ear. But when the clerk called his name, the farmer said nothing. The clerk said his name again. Nothing. The clerk marked him as not voting and moved on.

Now the sound of women crying was audible from above.

Walker's was the final name on the legislature roster. When the clerk said his name, he stood tall and shouted a triumphant, "No!"

Again it was a tie. The amendment was done for.

Then Banks Turner pushed back in his chair, stood, and filled the stunned silence. "Mr. Speaker," he said haltingly, "I wish to be recorded as voting Aye."

And with that, the Tennessee statehouse exploded.

Suffs unpinned their roses and threw them in the air so that yellow flowers rained on the men below. Leaning out the window of her hotel, Catt heard the roar. She saw women in yellow running downhill in her direction and knew they'd won at long last.

Strong-arm political tactics from the governor had likely redirected a reluctant Banks Turner, who in the end had voted consistently from tabling to ratification. The truly galling about-face had come from Harry Burn, who'd worn a red rose for all to see. Insults and threats poured in from all sides.

The sergeant at arms rushed to protect him from the crowd while Burn raced through the clerk's room and out a window, along a ledge, back through an open window of the legislative library, then out into the street, where he kept running.

★ ★ ★

The following day, Harry Burn was back in the capitol, no rose in sight, but wearing a tie in suffragist white. He read a prepared statement on the floor of the house, where among other things he stated without embarrassment or apology, "I knew that a mother's advice is always safest for a boy to follow, and my mother wanted me to vote for ratification."

He might have looked up from his speech then and into the faces filling the seats above, before going on, "I appreciated the fact that an opportunity such as seldom comes to mortal man to free seventeen million women from political slavery was mine."

Motherhood, that tired tool of the Antis, that stick against women, had won the day for women's suffrage.

★ ★ ★

While millions of women may have been "freed" with ratification of the Nineteenth Amendment on August 18, 1920, it wasn't nearly enough. Not in terms of numbers, nor in action.

While many white women benefited from winning the vote in 1920, many women of color couldn't vote for years, even decades, to come. Native Americans had to wait until

passage of the Indian Citizenship Act of 1924 (which did not ensure voting rights state by state), while Chinese immigrants couldn't become citizens until 1943. For Indian immigrants full rights didn't come until 1946, and for Japanese immigrants it wasn't until 1952. Legal protection for African American voters didn't come until the Voting Rights Act of 1965. And racial injustice around voting continues to this day.

Given such suppression of voting rights, it may be no surprise that it took until the 1960s for women to vote in the same numbers as men nationally. But also, without the unifying fight for suffrage, women lost a central struggle to rally around.

From 1920 onward, the fight for women to find their voices, and raise them, became increasingly fractured and complex, though no less essential.

So hereafter, nine ways of looking at women speaking out in America. A far from comprehensive, but thoroughly fabulous, chorus.

CHAPTER 11

WOMEN ARE PEOPLE TOO: BETTY FRIEDAN

Prior to the 1940s and 1950s, a woman was condemned if she did not do what was expected of her. In the 1950s, she was pitied if she did not *want* what was expected of her.

STEPHANIE COONTZ
A STRANGE STIRRING: THE FEMININE MYSTIQUE AND AMERICAN WOMEN AT THE DAWN OF THE 1960S

IN THE SPRING OF SEVENTH GRADE I went to bed and didn't get up for a long time. About six weeks. The previous fall, 1979, I'd started junior high, where a girl I'd always considered my closest friend attained popular new friends by publicly noting my messy hair, buck teeth, and bad fashion. I went from thinking of myself as mostly a pretty good athlete and student to finding out I was ugly, uncool, and only smart in ways that didn't matter. Or did matter, but as a social liability.

One day in the cafeteria I mentioned to a girl foolish enough to sit with me that I got how a person might want to kill herself. She rolled her eyes and said I just wanted attention. To be fair, I heard this a lot.

I took to my bed. Day after long day I watched light filter across the alfalfa fields and through my attic bedroom window, pink dawn to pink dusk. I was lonely, and bored. At some point I located a small black-and-white television my brother had won years before at the 1974 Montana State Spelling Bee. TVs weren't allowed in our rooms, but what could my parents do? Ground me?

I loved *The Incredible Hulk* (transforming rage, check) and *Battlestar Galactica* (outer space, that comforting distance), but watched daytime talk shows through to evening news with the same brainless attention. Until one night I saw a kind of woman I'd never seen on TV before. She was short and solid, with a largish nose. Not young or especially pretty,

but stylish and at ease. She was smart, loud, angry, and witty. The sideburned man interviewing her listened with attention when she spoke. I crawled across the mattress for a better look. At the bottom of the screen it said: Betty Friedan.

Bathed in blue television light, I suddenly experienced a Caravaggio-like moment of revelation: I didn't have to be pretty and perfect to become a woman who mattered. I could be loud and smart and pissed off. I didn't even need to be liked. Something shifted. I was going to be OK.

★ ★ ★

I NEVER FORGOT HER NAME, but it was years before I knew who Betty Friedan was. Many more before I finally read *The Feminine Mystique*, the book that made her famous. Oddly, my own experience with Friedan was a lot like that of her book's first readers in 1963. A flash of recognition and insight, followed by hope. Her first chapter, "The Problem That Has No Name," begins: "The problem lay buried, unspoken, for many years in the minds of American women. It was a strange stirring, a sense of dissatisfaction, a yearning that women suffered in the middle of the twentieth century in the United States. Each suburban housewife struggled with it alone." Speaking mostly to isolated and depressed middle-class women filled with shame for having such feelings, Friedan's book said, you are not alone. Also, it's not you, it's the system. And the system sucks.

The title itself named an unspoken ideal of womanhood that permeated the culture,

a twentieth-century paradigm akin to the "separate spheres" of the nineteenth. What had once been a "natural law" grounded in Christianity was by the early sixties based on Freudian psychology. Both insisted there was a recipe for how men and women must act if they are to be happy (read: normal).

The feminine mystique Friedan was disassembling embodied all the things women were told (and many believed) they needed to be fulfilled: a husband, children, a two-car garage, a cute figure, and a sparkling clean home. Anything else—freedom, creativity, autonomy, a career, money, whatever—led to neuroses, narcissism, frigidity, and madness. Also it made your sons gay, potentially schizophrenic, even autistic.

Freidan's book took stock and called bullshit. She offered history, statistics, and clear logical thinking. And she pointed out a then profound idea, stated explicitly in the title of the original 1960 *Good Housekeeping* article that became her book: "Women Are People Too."

The Feminine Mystique spoke to the first generation of women who started families after World War II. Their grandmothers had fought for the right to vote and to attend universities, while their mothers, and maybe even they themselves, had worked outside the home during World War II. But after the war was over came a strange acquiescence and reversal. Women went home and stayed there.

Friedan laid out the problem in the first chapter: Women were going backward. "The proportion of women attending college in comparison to men dropped from 47 percent in 1920 to 35 percent in 1958," and "By the mid-fifties 60 percent dropped out of college to marry, or because they were afraid too much education would be a marriage bar." Friedan blamed this retreat on women's magazines, consumerism, Freudian psychology, and the stress of the Cold War. But she didn't let women off the hook. She insisted women needed to take up their own lives.

She tried to motivate by inspiration. In a chapter titled "The Passionate Journey," Friedan shared an abridged history of suffragism (we're never done retelling that story) but warned that passage of the Nineteenth Amendment was just a start, and a false one at that. It had lulled women into believing they were done. "To women born after 1920, feminism was dead history. It ended as a vital movement in America with the winning of that final right: the vote."

For white feminism that may have been true, but as noted earlier, "the vote" was hardly available to everyone in 1920, much less all women.

★ ★ ★

FRIEDAN WAS CERTAINLY AWARE of America's inequities. Born Bettye Goldstein, "a nice Jewish girl" in Peoria, Illinois, Friedan said her lifelong passion for justice came from early experiences of anti-Semitism. In high school she'd wanted to join a school sorority but, she said, "being Jewish, you didn't get into a sorority." She spent much of her adolescence isolated from her peers. "I really didn't want to spend an Emily Dickinson adolescence reading poetry on gravestones," she said, but that's what happened.

Friedan got into Smith College—her mother's dream for her—where she was editor of the school newspaper. She turned it markedly political with articles about domestic workers trying to unionize on campus and the like. After college she flirted with Marxism and wrote for labor publications. As a young wife and mother in the early 1950s, Friedan lived in Queens, where neighbors in her housing development included local civil rights leaders. But in 1956, the Friedans moved to a mostly white New York suburb. While she was hardly your average frustrated housewife, Friedan understood those suburban women well, their anxieties and longings. Through successive drafts, *The Feminine Mystique* homed in on their struggles.

★ ★ ★

THE BOOK'S PUBLICATION is often credited with kicking off the "second wave" of American feminism, though, of course, history is never so simple. And if credit is going around, it should include the messy truth that *The Feminine Mystique* is written for and about educated, middle-class white women.

Friedan does mention Sojourner Truth (quoting Gage's famous but invented passage) and abolitionism, but offers only passing mention of the contemporary civil rights movement. The year before Friedan's book came out, Dolores Huerta co-founded the National Farm Workers Association in California, while Fannie Lou Hamer, who would speak with eloquent rage at the 1964 Democratic National Convention, was beaten and jailed in Mississippi for even attempting to register to vote as a black woman. While Friedan railed against white women's passivity, Huerta, Hamer, and Rosa Parks toiled on the front lines of the struggle for equal rights.

But for many women, Friedan's book was a bomb. It blew out the cobwebs of complacency and lit a fire under millions of lives. It made Friedan famous—and, presumably, rich—around the world. The book sold 60,000 in hardback (good sales even today) and 1.5 million in paperback. It has sold many more copies since and has been credited, or blamed, for much of women's rights history that followed. (In 2005, the conservative publication *Human Events* listed *The Feminine Mystique* at number seven on its list of the Ten Most Harmful Books of the Nineteenth and Twentieth Centuries.

Number one was *The Communist Manifesto*, followed by *Mein Kampf*.)

Famous (and infamous) by the mid-sixties, Friedan might have ridden the coattails of her first book forever. Certainly she might have aimed to write another bestseller. But, she said, "I realized that it was not enough to write a book. There had to be social change." While attending a 1966 federal conference on the status of women, Friedan and a group of other politically engaged women met in her hotel room with the idea of creating an organization like the NAACP, but for women's rights. The group included lawyers, spiritual leaders, and political leaders like Shirley Chisholm, who would be the first black woman elected to Congress and the first black candidate for

president. During their brainstorming, Friedan grabbed a paper napkin and wrote NOW.

The National Organization for Women (NOW) still advocates for equality in every area of society, from reproductive rights to fair pay to safety in the home. It pushed for passage of the Equal Rights Amendment (ERA)—which Alice Paul had spearheaded after ratification of the Nineteenth Amendment. NOW gave defining legal names to gender crimes like sexual harassment and domestic violence, and by naming them helped women speak out.

* * *

FRIEDAN LOST NONE OF HER prickly indignity with age. In 2000, I was pregnant with my second child and struggling to get through a long day with my first, a toddler, when I heard her on our local NPR station. The interviewer,

a man, asked about infighting in the seventies feminist movement. That fast, Friedan called him divisive and sexist and called off the interview. I stood in my kitchen, eyes wide, then lowered my girth onto a chair, laughing.

Was it fair to call him sexist? I don't know. Was she wrong? Maybe. But it felt great to hear a woman go ahead and get mad. To say fuck off and mean it.

CHAPTER 12

PICTURE THIS

The fault lies not in our stars, our hormones, our menstrual cycles, or empty internal spaces, but in our institutions and our education.

LINDA NOCHLIN, "WHY HAVE THERE BEEN NO GREAT WOMEN ARTISTS?" 1971

IN THE FALL OF 1969, art historian Linda Nochlin had just resumed teaching at her alma mater, Vassar College, when an acquaintance dropped by "with a briefcase full of polemical literature." Specifically, feminist rags of a type we'd later call zines—i.e., cheaply made, ranty, bursting with energy and passion.

Nochlin wasn't interested. "I already was a liberated woman," she wrote years later, "and I knew enough about feminism—suffragettes and such—to realize that we, in 1969, were beyond such things." But to appease her acquaintance, Nochlin accepted the tracts and somehow, after tucking in her newborn daughter, Daisy, and doing the last of the dinner dishes and getting her grading done and preparing her classes and who knows what else, she started to read. By two A.M.

she had "cartoonish light bulbs going off in my head at a frantic pace." Art history would never be the same.

A few weeks later she posted a notice on Vassar's art history bulletin board alerting students that she was creating a new seminar: The Image of Women in the Nineteenth and Twentieth Centuries. This included women as models, prostitutes, fallen women, and mothers (sometimes both), but also women artists themselves.

As far as Western art history goes, Italian Giorgio Vasari had kicked things off by basically founding the field in 1550 with his *The Lives of the Most Excellent Painters, Sculptors, and Architects.* Out of some 160 artists, Vasari included four women, actually far better stats than most art history books to come. But now, after more than four hundred years of Western art history, women quite suddenly mattered. Women were now significant both as subjects and as artists because Professor Nochlin believed they were and was conducting her seminar on them. (Or at least women mattered in an insular, academic world of less than two thousand students in podunk Poughkeepsie, New York.)

Nochlin's small revolutionary act might've remained a Vassar secret if not for a commencement address there by journalist and feminist Gloria Steinem the following spring.

It was the first time Steinem had given a public talk on her own and she was, she said later, "terrified." Professionally, she was best known for a 1962 piece on "the Pill" and—more infamously—for a widely read article called "A Bunny's Tale," in which she'd gone undercover as one of Hugh Hefner's Playboy Bunnies at a Manhattan club and wrote about how, believe it or not, the work wasn't so fun for the women wearing cottontails. She'd been honing her activism skills since, going on the road to speak about women's rights alongside African American activists Margaret Sloan, Flo Kennedy, and Dorothy Pitman Hughes.

Steinem was fast becoming the face of American feminism, at least in part because she had a very pretty one. Her legs were likewise famous. Her first editor and mentor at *New York* magazine, Clay Felker, told the *Washington Post* that he discovered Steinem when, "I saw her standing outside my office one day. . . . I thought she had great legs." To be fair, he also said, "I gave her her first bylined assignment and it was excellent." But Steinem

was noticeably attractive and that made her interesting (to the mainstream) and suspect (to many feminists).

Nochlin likely knew all of this when she sank into her seat that day to hear Steinem speak. I like to picture her in big sunglasses, shading her face with a pale hand, sensible but stylish shoes a bit wet from the grass. She might have glanced at her watch a few times. Her husband, Richard Pommer, also taught at Vassar—maybe he was beside her—so baby Daisy would be with a sitter. She might have smiled when Steinem walked to the podium, skirt shorter than typical at Vassar, wondering what a firebrand feminist might say to a group of fairly placid undergraduates, many of whom would wield their excellent degrees to marvelous effect as, say—per Nochlin decades later—"head of the PTA in Wilkes-Barre, Pennsylvania." It was 1970, but not enough had changed.

Also in the audience were Nochlin's friends, attorney Brenda Feigen (also a friend of Steinem's), and Feigen's brother Richard, an art dealer. Steinem proclaimed 1970 "the year of Women's Liberation," then bashed the quality of her own education at Smith College (where she said that even a women's college had somehow forgotten to mention women in history), then name-dropped the Black Panthers and recommended certain of their methods. Enthralled, Richard Feigen turned to Nochlin and said, "Linda, I would love to show women artists, but I can't find any good ones. Why are there no great women artists?"

Why are there no great women artists?
Lightbulb.
Or even: Hair on fire.

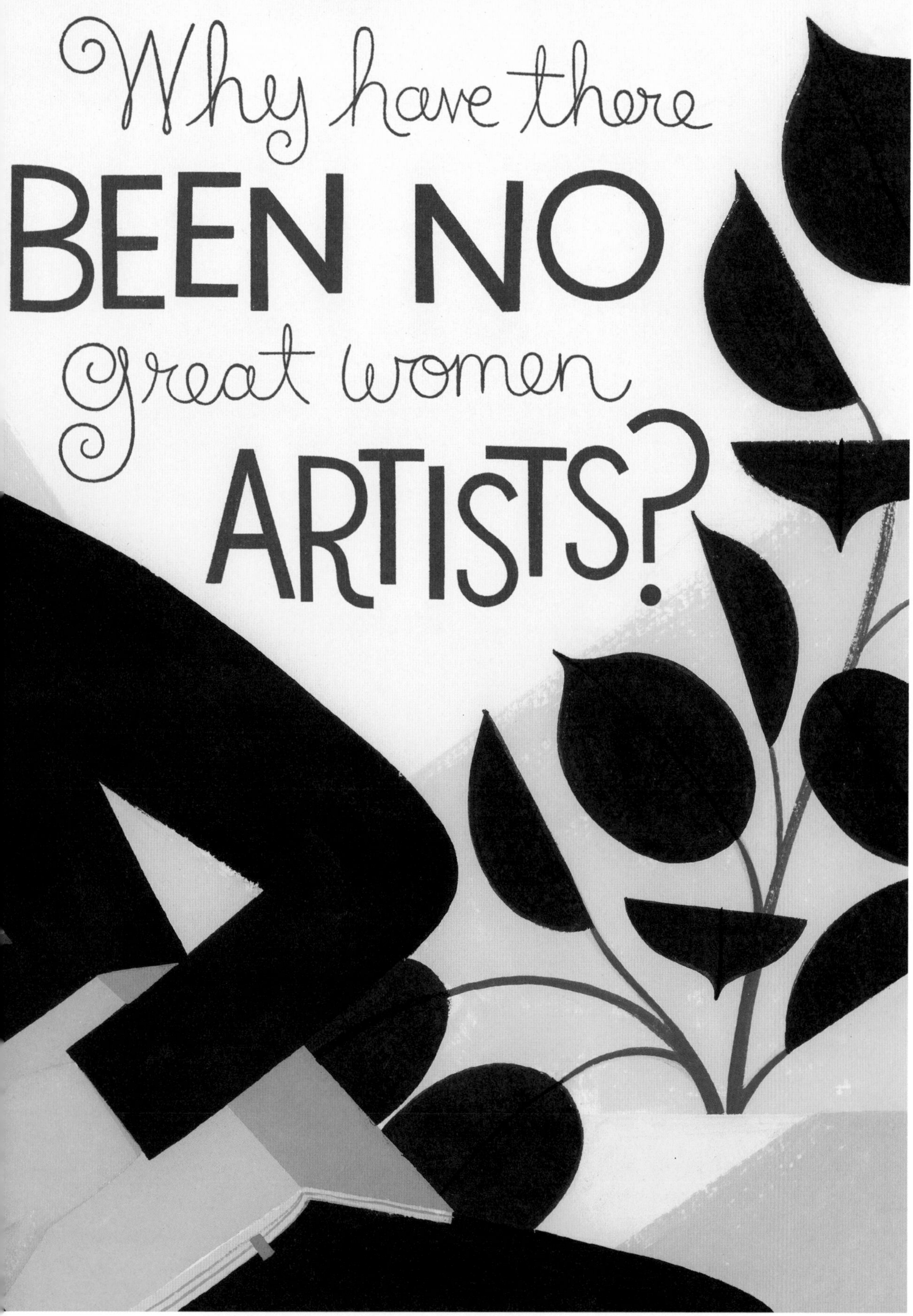
Why have there
BEEN NO
great women
ARTISTS?

I'll confess that when referencing Richard Feigen to myself, I use the diminutive Dick. But he can hardly be blamed for asking the question. Even Nochlin, who'd spent the past months teaching and researching and thinking about the topic of women and art, had no ready answer. "I went home and thought about this issue for days," she wrote. "It haunted me."

By the end of that year she'd written a 4,000-word, impeccably argued, thoroughly reasoned and wry response to a question that had lived mostly unspoken. In "Why Have There Been No Great Women Artists?" Nochlin systematically elucidated, top to bottom, all the ways women had been denied access to the education and institutions that made pursuing serious art possible. Then she went a step further and questioned the whole patriarchal emperor-has-no-clothes mythology around "greatness."

Nochlin's essay was intended for feminist writer Vivian Gornick's forceful collection, *Women in Sexist Society*, but an editor friend of Nochlin's got wind of it and also nabbed it for the January 1971 *ArtNews*, a special issue dedicated to "Women's Liberation, Women Artists, and Art History."

With that, feminist art history was born.

Nochlin's essay was an object lesson for how self and history could prove the recipe for something thrillingly new. As that pithy feminist saying goes: *The personal is political.*

Nochlin was, she realized, uniquely situated—personally (woman, wife, and mother), politically (feminist), professionally (professor of art history at a renowned institution)—to take on the structural inequities of Western art history and begin to dismantle them. Whew, that sounds hella boring. But Nochlin, for all her intellectual rigor, was witty and charming. Her essay lit readers up with the same cartoon lightbulbs that had gone off in her own brain a year earlier.

In example after example, Nochlin explained how pictures tell stories we don't even realize we're being told. Stories about how women are forever subjects, even objects. As such, however beautiful and supposedly adored and put on pedestals and worshipped and petted, women are powerless. They are, in effect, Hefner bunnies. Cute and cuddly sex objects shoved into painful shoes.

★ ★ ★

IN OCTOBER 1971, ten months after Nochlin's essay ran in *ArtNews*, mainstream glossy *Esquire* featured Gloria Steinem and co-activist Dorothy Pitman Hughes standing in a single pair of giant pants, right arms raised in what by then everyone recognized as the Black Power salute. White and black, they were beautiful badass poster girls for revolution. This was a picture so powerful that the Smithsonian acquired the original for its permanent collection. So iconic that I just realized I'm wearing a T-shirt with the same picture on it as I write this.

Images of women were suddenly changing. And so were magazines.

By 1970, women's magazines had been around forever. They were a big part of what Betty Friedan complained about in *The Feminine Mystique*. Pandering to women (what color to paint your nails or hair; what food to make sweet hubby when he gets home from work dog-tired and starving; what dress or bra or scarf he might like best) with articles often written by women, so-called "women's magazines" were almost always run by male editors. Then on March 18, 1970, a hundred women staged a sit-in at *Ladies' Home Journal* to demand they install a woman editor in chief. Even radical feminists like Vivian Gornick (her again), a fiery writer I can hardly imagine on the same planet as *Ladies' Home Journal*, called the sit-in "a watershed moment. It showed us, the activists in the women's movement, that we did, indeed, have a movement."

Right about the time Nochlin's essay appeared in that special 1971 "women's" issue of *ArtNews* (edited by a man, Thomas Hess), Steinem and Brenda Feigen (her again) hosted a pair of meetings in their apartments to drum up interest in creating a new women-run publication. Both nights the rooms were filled with women writers, journalists, and activists. Some didn't like the idea of going mainstream with feminism, while others—like Feigen and Steinem and Pitman Hughes—thought a slick magazine on women's issues was the perfect sugared pill to turn American women on to women's lib.

Clay Felker, Steinem's boss at *New York* magazine (the one who'd first admired her legs), offered to launch the new magazine as an insert in *New York*'s December issue, which basically funded the first issue. Game on. Except, what to call it? *Sojourner* (as in Truth) was an early choice, but people thought it sounded like a travel magazine; *Sisters* sounded like the articles might be about nuns. A friend

of Steinem's suggested a term she'd recently heard about on the radio: *Ms.*

In case you are unaware, until recently women in the English-speaking world lacked an honorific not specifically linked to marital status. Men had Mr. (same whether married or unmarried), while women had Miss (unmarried) or Mrs. (married, followed by husband's surname). In short, there was no way to be one's own woman. Even a married woman named Jane Doe who kept her "maiden name" (a phrase that itself speaks volumes) could be neither Miss Doe (meaning "unmarried") nor Mrs. Doe (meaning married to Mr. Doe).

Ms. magazine immediately telegraphed *feminist*, and *new*, and *for all women*. It also helped promote use of the new honorific, so that already by early 1972, "Ms." was approved for official government documents and even showed up in the American Heritage Dictionary. But it took far longer for most institutions. Not until June 20, 1986, did the *New York Times* stop asking women their marital status and print "Ms." instead. It had taken street protests starting in 1974 all the way up to shareholder activism in the 1980s to get the *Times* to get with the times.

Back to "women's magazines," Madison Avenue had been convinced that American women were only interested in articles about shiny hair and shiny floors. But the first issue of *Ms.* sold out all 300,000 copies in just three days, leading to a healthy 26,000 subscriptions. It featured a wide range of content, including poetry by Sylvia Plath and articles from "On Raising Kids Without Sex Roles" to "The Housewife's Moment of Truth," to its boldest foray, "Women Tell the Truth about Their Abortions."

★ ★ ★

WOMEN HAD OF COURSE been having abortions for a long time. They'd been legal in the United States until the late nineteenth century, and weren't even banned by the Catholic Church until 1869. *Ms.* wanted to make it acceptable for women to talk about what they'd chosen for their own bodies, just as abortion was poised to become a pivotal political issue. One year later, *Roe v. Wade* again legalized abortion in America and became the flashpoint of culture wars to come.

The first *Ms.* cover did not feature a skinny model (per *Vogue*) or a sweetly smiling housewife (*Ladies' Home Journal*). Instead its inaugural cover featured artwork depicting the Indian goddess Kali—mother of the whole universe—as a mythical and many-armed housewife. Blue skinned, per tradition, but bearing in her eight arms, clockwise from lower left, an iron, a steering wheel, a mirror, a telephone, a clock, a flaming feather duster, a frying pan, and a typewriter. Managing all of it, the goddess balances on one foot in yogic Tree Pose, in red heels, while fat tears drip from both eyes. If all that's not enough, a baby visibly glows in her belly. Mother of the universe as universal housewife. Doing it all, but also overwhelmed.

Cultural appropriation? Pretty much, but also a pretty brilliant summation of the eternal challenges of womanhood across cultures, race, and time. Kali was, in Steinem's words, "racially 'multibiguous.'" She embraced multitudes.

Ms. magazine embodied a whole new view on life: the female perspective. See ya, male gaze.

★ ★ ★

THE FIRST ISSUE OF *MS.* was staring out from newsstands as Nochlin conducted a session of the 1972 College Art Association in San Francisco titled "Eroticism and Female Imagery in Nineteenth-Century Art." In her introduction, Nochlin quickly indicated how representations of women are empirically different from depictions of men. To prove her point, she used a nineteenth-century photo she'd found in a "book of demi-porn I had bought at a bookstall on the quai in Paris

the previous summer." Called *Buy My Apples*, it depicted a mostly naked woman (still wearing black stockings and boots) with her breasts resting on a tray of apples she holds against her chest. It's frankly not unlike Gauguin's famous *Women with Mango Blossoms* (also known as *Two Tahitian Women*) in the Metropolitan Museum of Art. High vs. low art, what's porn and what's art, that's the direction Nochlin might have been expected to go with the topic. But she was just getting started.

Nochlin had looked for a male version of such nudes, but finding nothing decided to create one herself. She'd intended to utilize "a frankfurter—kosher, of course." But at an earlier meeting of women in the arts she'd explained her idea to French-born sculptor Louise Bourgeois, who instantly got it. "Use a banana instead," Bourgeois counseled. "It will make the point better."

So Nochlin made an appointment with the Vassar art department's male model and met him in the studio with a tray, some bananas, and a Nikon. She showed him the nineteenth-century photograph. He disrobed, cleverly keeping on his hiking socks and "shit-kickers" while holding the tray of bananas well below his waist. *Buy My Bananas* was born.

Compare and contrast.

★ ★ ★

"IT WAS THE ONLY 'SERIOUS' PHOTO I ever took," Nochlin wrote in 2012. "The rest is art history."

PAIA,
MAUI

UNITED STATES CONGRESS

N

WOMEN'S
RIGHTS
ARE
HUMAN RIGHTS

PATSY T. MINK
EQUAL
OPPORTUNITY
IN
EDUCATION
ACT

HONOLULU,
O'AHU

CHAPTER 13

—=13=—

RUNNING STRONG:
PATSY MATSU TAKEMOTO MINK

No person in the United States shall, on the basis of sex, be excluded from participation in, be denied the benefits of, or be subjected to discrimination under any education program or activity receiving federal financial assistance.

TITLE IX OF THE EDUCATION AMENDMENTS OF 1972

THE SEVENTIETH RUNNING of the Boston Marathon—April 19, 1967— was both cold and wet. Sleet and gusty winds had nineteen-year-old Syracuse University student Kathrine Switzer second-guessing her outfit. She gave up the burgundy running set she'd carefully ironed for the event and instead pinned her race number to her oversize gray sweatshirt. She kept her big cotton sweatpants on, too. In the starting area, she looked a lot like the men shaking out and trying to stay warm all around her, wiry and anxious and ready to run. Only lipstick and earrings gave her away, but at first, nobody much noticed her.

She'd signed up for the marathon after convincing her mentor, fifty-year-old campus mailman and Boston veteran Arnie Briggs, that a woman could run 26.2 miles without her uterus becoming impaired or

some other physical catastrophe. Convincing him had required a thirty-one-mile "test" run just weeks before. Switzer's reproductive organs still intact and Arnie physically spent, he gave her the greenlight to enter the Boston Marathon.

The marathon registration form looked straightforward enough. Switzer checked all the appropriate boxes, paid the three-buck fee (you read that right), and signed her name like always: K. V. Switzer. It never occurred to her this might be considered duplicitous.

Now she was lined up alongside Arnie, their friend John, and her boyfriend, Big Tom Miller, who'd registered last minute and hadn't trained. But as a former All-American in football and current Olympic hopeful in the hammer throw, he figured he could do whatever scrawny old Arnie and wispy Kathrine could. "If a girl can run a marathon, I can run a marathon," he'd said, with the smug certainty of the clueless.

Of the 741 runners that day, Switzer was the only registered female. No official noticed her as she entered her corral.

The men around her, eventually realizing she was a she, asked if Switzer really planned to run the whole thing and gave her a thumbs-up when she said of course. One guy had his wife snap a picture. A girl running a marathon! Too crazy!

The first couple of miles were a blast, everyone excited and Switzer thrilled to be running a legendary marathon as her first. Arnie and Big Tom beamed as other men cheered her on. She smiled, too, happy to be there and trusting her training. When a press truck pushed through and photographers on the back started snapping pictures, the friends waved back, laughing. But suddenly there was the unmistakable sound of leather slapping pavement and someone yelling. Startled, Switzer turned in time to see the enraged face of a man lunging for her, shouting in a Scottish brogue, "Get the hell out of my race and give me those numbers!" Arnie recognized race director Jock Semple, grabbed his arm, and shouted for him to leave the girl alone. Semple threw him off, grabbed Switzer by the sweatshirt, and held on. She was trapped, fully stopped, so scared and startled she peed herself a little.

Jock Semple may have been a furious Scot capable of shaking off a skinny fifty-year-old distance runner and holding onto a writhing young woman, but he was no match for a 235-pound former football star. Big Tom threw a body block that sent Semple

airborne. Seeing his body crumple at the side of the road, Switzer was afraid he might be dead (he wasn't). "Run!" Tom yelled. She did. Through it all, men hanging off the press truck kept shooting.

Switzer ran without stopping for twenty-four more miles, finishing long before her boyfriend, who had to walk. Clocking in at four hours and twenty minutes, Kathrine Switzer became the first woman to officially run the Boston Marathon. Stunned reporters—some plenty irritated for having to wait for her in the cold—peppered her with questions at the finish line, including, oddly, "Are you a suffragette?"

★ ★ ★

MAYBE PATSY MINK SAW the infamous photos of Switzer's Boston Marathon attack in newspapers the following day. But even if she missed them, she couldn't have missed what that run meant to women. Mink had been paving the way for strong women like Switzer for years, and after Switzer's win, Mink would carpet it.

Born in Hawaii in 1927, Patsy Matsu Takemoto Mink turned fourteen the day after the bombing of Pearl Harbor. It was a bad time to be of Japanese descent, but that didn't stop her from assembling a voting coalition at her school and becoming the first female student body president at Maui High a month later. Unlike many Japanese Americans, Mink's family was never interned. She went on to become high school valedictorian, then president of the Pre-Med Students Club at the University of Hawaii, where she was a dual major in zoology and chemistry. Driven and ambitious, she was what, today, we might call a gunner. But none of some twenty medical schools she applied to after college saw her that way. In 1948 not a single American medical school would admit a woman.

"It was the most devastating disappointment of my life," Mink said years later, "that I could have spent my whole educational experience, you know, geared toward one thing and then have all the schools I wrote say 'no, can't have you.'" Mink had to give up her dream of med school. She pivoted, applying to law schools as a consolation prize. She might have faced the same outcome had the University of Chicago not admitted her under its "foreign quota" (for an intellectual powerhouse, they were surprisingly unaware of Hawaii's status as a territory of the United States). Mink was one of two women in her law school class.

By 1951 she had her JD and a new marriage, but no law firm would hire her. She went back to working in the law library, the same job she'd had as a student. In 1952 she had a baby and moved back to Hawaii, where she, a third-generation Hawaiian who'd graduated from the University of Hawaii, wasn't allowed to take the bar exam because her husband was from Pennsylvania and married women had to assume their husband's residency status. She challenged the statute on grounds of sexism (in 1952!), won, passed the bar, and—surprise—still no firm would hire her. So she opened up a solo private practice in Honolulu. Her first client paid her in fish.

At this point you might be asking: How much more can a person take? Mink, it turns out, could take quite a lot. She saw her career as a marathon, not a sprint. She could identify with any long-distance runner, especially one like Kathrine Switzer, for whom obstacles were things to shrug off, elude, outrun, not things that would stop her in her tracks.

Mink became involved in territorial politics, ran for some things and lost. But after Hawaii became the fiftieth state in 1959, she was made a delegate to the Democratic Convention of 1960, where she came to national attention for speaking passionately in support of civil rights as a cornerstone of the Democratic Party platform. Four years later she became the first woman of color elected to Congress.

That was just the beginning of Mink making history.

In the winter of 1970 she spoke before the Senate hearing committee for Judge George Harrold Carswell's nomination to the Supreme Court. Carswell was Nixon's second attempt at a Supreme Court nominee. Mink was the first witness to oppose him, on the pithy grounds that "Judge Carswell demonstrated a total lack of understanding of the concept of equality." She cited a case from the previous year, when Carswell was serving on the Fifth Circuit Court of Appeals and voted not to hear the case of a woman denied a job because she had young children. "His vote represented a vote against the right of women to be treated equally and fairly under the law," Mink told the Senate hearing, her voice no doubt edged with the sharp prick of personal experience.

Carswell was not confirmed.

That made way for Harry Blackmun to become Richard Nixon's finally approved appointee to the Supreme Court. Three years later it was Blackmun who authored the majority opinion in a pivotal little case called *Roe v. Wade*, prohibiting state and federal restrictions on abortion. Mink's objection to sexism helped make Blackmun possible.

★ ★ ★

BUT MINK'S GREATEST ACT in Congress was sponsoring and co-authoring Title IX of the 1972 Amendments to the Higher Education Act. Signed into law by Richard Nixon, Title IX guarantees the broad protection of sex in education—meaning you can't discriminate against women (or men) in any arena of federally funded educational pursuits, whether in the classroom or on the playing field. The impact of Title IX has been profound, nothing short of revolutionary.

In higher education, medical and law schools—which once nearly foiled Mink entirely—now graduate almost equal numbers of men and women. And where just one in twenty-seven high school girls played sports in 1972, today it's more like two in five. Since the passage of Title IX, the number of women playing college sports has increased over 600 percent.

In 2007, fifty years after her entry in the '67 Boston Marathon, Switzer ran it again to celebrate, this time alongside 13,297 other women (who'd beaten out thousands more to secure a spot). Progress. But it's not all roses, of course. Women's sports are still underfunded compared with men's at all levels, preschool to pro.

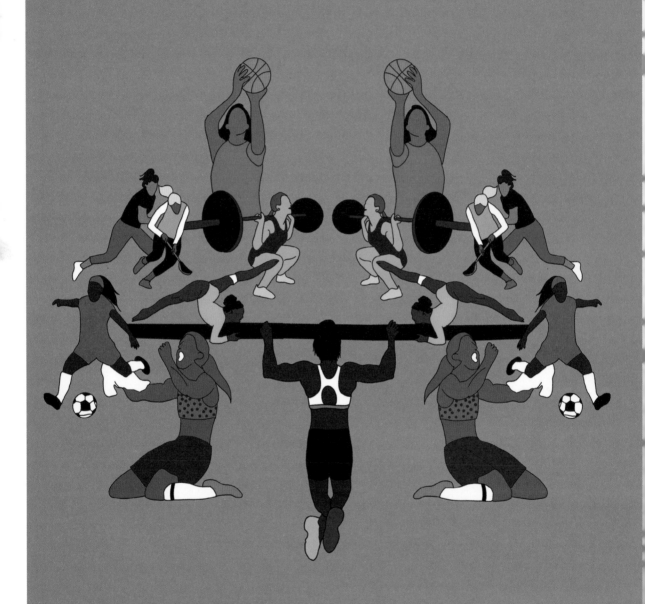

And women doctors and lawyers still make less than their male counterparts. That all needs work. If gunner Mink were still alive, she'd still be fighting inequity. She'd want us to push on to the finish line.

Mink died in office in 2002. Later that year, Congress renamed Title IX: The Patsy T. Mink Equal Opportunity in Education Act.

Just imagine what Mink might have cured had she gone to medical school.

The Black
Unicorn

Sister Outsider

A Burst of
Light

I Am Your Sister

Your Silence Will
Not Protect You

CHAPTER 14

LESBIANS & LIBERATION: AUDRE LORDE

The history of white women who are unable to hear Black women's words, or to maintain dialogue with us, is long and discouraging.

AUDRE LORDE, AN OPEN LETTER TO MARY DALY, 1979

HARLEM, NYC. 1939. Audrey Geraldine Lorde, the youngest of three sisters, sits at the kitchen table, writing out her name. The pencil is thin and hard to hold in her chubby hand. Just four years old, she can read and write already. She's proud of what she can do. Born literally tongue-tied (the actual medical condition) and so nearsighted she's nearly blind, Audrey already senses she is different from other people. Her mother senses it, too, and doesn't like it. This confuses Audrey and brings so many feelings at once that it's like standing in a rushing river trying to seize fish with her small hands. It's all so difficult. These many feelings, this hurt. Sometimes she just speaks in poems. Words from books she can read already. Words help.

She starts her name on the left side of the page, a big strong "A," then onward to the last gentle "e." She's skipped "Geraldine" on purpose because she doesn't care for it. She takes a long look. Sees she's forgotten the "y" in her first name again, that letter with the tricky tail slashing under everything. She doesn't like "y." She likes her name better just the way she's written it: Audre Lorde. *Symmetrical* isn't a word she knows yet, but *pleasing* is a word she understands well. This name is hers. It fits.

★ ★ ★

DECADES LATER LORDE WOULD WRITE in her "biomythography" *Zami: A New Spelling of My Name*, that at four years old she already felt "love" for "the evenness of AUDRELORDE." Much of what she cherished was all right there, from the beginning: naming, writing, self-regard, evenness.

Lorde's parents were immigrants from the West Indies, living in Harlem. Her father, Frederic Byron Lorde, went by his middle name, a perfect appellation for the father of a one-day-famous poet (*see* Lord Byron). But neither he nor Linda, Audre's mother, took much note of their youngest's burgeoning talent. They worked in real estate and were busy, busy. The Great Depression was still a fresh and terrifying wound, the thing that had stopped them from returning to their tropical island homeland. They were stuck instead on an urban island off the coast of America, where work was their one salvation. Three kids and two careers are a lot. A person only has two hands.

Lorde went to Catholic school, not the best atmosphere for a smart black queer girl given to honesty and poetics. Later, she got into Hunter College High School in Manhattan, a school for intellectually gifted students, and there joined what one critic calls a "sisterhood of rebels." Poets, naturally. She was literary editor of the school's arts journal, but that didn't stop them from rejecting one of her poems as "inappropriate." A little rag in town called *Seventeen* magazine published her poem instead.

Still a teenager, Lorde was a professionally published poet. Damn.

By 1970 she'd gotten a BA—with a year abroad at the National University of Mexico—and an MLS, and become a librarian and gotten married and had two children and gotten divorced and published her first book of poems and come out as a lesbian. It was the dawn of a new decade and Audre Lorde had been and was busy and brave. Being a black,

feminist, lesbian, mother, poet, warrior took immense energy, physical and emotional. "I am defined as *other* in every group I'm part of," she wrote, believing outsider status held "both strength and weakness."

Lorde was, in a very real sense, intersectionality embodied.

★ ★ ★

ABOUT THE LESBIANS. We haven't much discussed them here, and it's already 1970 and well over a hundred years from where we started, so we're probably overdue. But in June 1969 the Stonewall riots were the shot heard 'round the world for Gay Liberation, and by June 1970 the first Gay Pride Parades were held in New York, Chicago, Los Angeles, and San

Francisco in commemoration. So in a way, we're right on time.

Lesbians have of course always been part of women's history. In body and in rhetoric. Throughout the fight for suffrage, women in the cause were depicted as childless, masculine, unattractive, man-hating, and, you got it: lesbians. To work for suffrage was to get painted with that brush. In fact, becoming a suffragist might even turn a girl gay, if popular cartoons were to be believed. Fear of lesbians was just one more reason to fear feminists and to oppose what they stood for (hint: equality).

Even second-wave midwife Betty Friedan got in on the action. In *The Feminine Mystique* she fanned hetero fears about "the homosexuality that is spreading like a murky smog

over the American scene." Then in 1969, as head of NOW (the National Organization for Women), Friedan ran up a flag, warning fellow feminists about the clear and present danger of the "Lavender Menace." With the lesbian albatross around feminism's neck, Friedan warned, women's liberation could not hope for mainstream acceptance.

Lesbians were understandably annoyed that a whole class of women might be blamed for sinking the feminist movement. So in May 1970, at the Second Congress to Unite Women in New York City, they underscored the fallacy in hetero vs. homo hysteria. Their guerrilla stunt involved cutting the lights and mics, then springing them back on to reveal seventeen women wearing Lavender Menace purple T-shirts—including bestselling novelist Rita Mae Brown—and carrying signs proclaiming: WOMEN'S LIBERATION IS A LESBIAN PLOT. That, among other amusing declarations. Lesbians were here, they were queer, and it was time second-wave feminism got used to it.

While the Lavender Menace used humor, Audre Lorde employed poetry. Which is to say that she created art that moved and changed people. In 1973, she published "Love Poem" in *Ms.* magazine, which included unmistakable lines like "when I entered her," along with tongues and breasts and navels and hips and flowing honey. Even the most obtuse reader couldn't miss the point. With "Love Poem" and others, Lorde wasn't just bringing lesbian love into the light, she was celebrating it. And her eroticism was meant to be shared — with all women, straight or gay. A transformative gift.

Lorde's revolution extended to teaching, to activism, to motherhood, to sisterhood, and

to civil rights. She lived intersectionality, a word that wouldn't be part of feminism until attorney and academic Kimberlé Crenshaw introduced it in 1989. Today it's a cornerstone of feminist thought, basically describing the many arenas of discrimination that overlap and inform us, be it race, gender, class, ethnicity, disability, age, etc. But in the 1970s it was simply Lorde's whole life, and mission.

It seemed like Lorde was everywhere then, including in the Combahee River Collective, a Boston-based group of black feminist lesbians confronting all the ways white feminism was not open to them, not helping them, and not acknowledging their needs. Founded in 1974 and named after a brilliant Civil War military campaign led by Harriet Tubman (that I highly recommend you look up), the CRC self-consciously connected their work to black women of the past. Their formal statement of purpose is a document as essential to twentieth- and twenty-first-century feminism as the Declaration of Rights and Sentiments was to the nineteenth. A sample line: "We realize that the only people who care enough about us to work consistently for our liberation is us. Our politics evolve from a healthy love for ourselves, our sisters, and our community which allows us to continue our struggle and work."

Audre Lorde embraced that love and shared it by writing, teaching, organizing, and reaching out to women all over the world. As a visiting professor in Berlin, she helped coin the term (and movement) *Afro-German*. She helped create Sisterhood in Support of Sisters in South Africa, for black women living under apartheid. She published dozens of books of poetry, essays, and autobiography.

In 1977, she was chosen to speak at the Modern Language Association Conference in Chicago. Spotlighted at center stage, she announced she'd recently undergone surgery for a breast tumor, a biopsy that required a three-week wait to find out if she'd live or die. The procedure had gotten her thinking about her life and shuffling through her regrets, she told the audience. I imagine her pausing in this moment, casting her gaze over the fidgeting men and women in that Midwest auditorium, safely seated in the shadows at the edge of the stage, living their mostly conventional lives (membership in the Modern Language Association notwithstanding).

"What I most regretted," Lorde said, "were my silences."

Then she talked about the community of women who supported her, about finding her voice, and strength. She went on: "Perhaps for some of you here today, I am the face of one of your fears. Because I am a woman, because I am Black, because I am lesbian, because I am myself—a Black woman warrior poet doing my work—come to ask you, are you doing yours?"

Damn. Great question.

CHAPTER 15

FIRST PERSON FEMALE

SOMETIMES I JUST SAY THAT MANKILLER IS MY NAME, I EARNED IT, AND I LET 'EM WONDER.

WILMA MANKILLER, PRINCIPAL CHIEF, CHEROKEE NATION

JUST HALFWAY THROUGH THE DECADE, the 1980s were already full of firsts for American women:

1981. Sandra Day O'Connor became the first female Supreme Court Justice. She told President Reagan, who'd appointed her, that abortion was "personally repugnant," but she kept personal feeling admirably apart from judicial dealing, and in twenty-five years on the court, she never voted to overturn *Roe v. Wade*.

1983. Sally Ride went from Stanford physics PhD to the first American woman in space (and first lesbian, so far as we know). Named to the Space Shuttle *Challenger* crew, her biggest obstacle may have been now familiar but asinine questions about the readiness of her reproductive organs for outer space. (Hint: ready for liftoff.)

1984. Joan Benoit became the first-ever women's Olympic marathon gold medalist. As of this writing, her time of 2:24:52 still stands as the American women's record for the Olympic marathon. In announcing Benoit's groundbreaking triumph over Norwegian legend Grete Waitz in Los Angeles, the *New York Times* helpfully referenced the athletes as Miss Benoit and Mrs. Waitz, respectively. Always good to know who's married and who's not in such situations.

That same summer, on July 19, 1984, Geraldine Ferraro—scrappy, Bronx-raised elementary school teacher turned attorney, then New York legislator—took the stage at the Democratic National Convention in San Francisco to become the first major party woman candidate for vice president in U.S. history. "I stand before you to proclaim

tonight, America is the land where dreams can come true, for all of us," a poised but exuberant Ferraro announced—to wild cheers. The convention hall was filled floor-to-rafters. Women shook signs that read like mash notes: "To Gerry with Love." Some cried. It had only been six years since Ferraro won a seat in Congress, after rising from beginnings that made such attainment plenty unlikely. On convention night, it seemed like the cheering for a woman wearing pearls and suffragist white might go on forever.

The veep nomination was a definite high-water mark in history, but said water was still plenty murky. On convention night and onward, the optics were being newly crafted for male presidential candidate Walter Mondale and his female running mate, Geraldine Ferraro. How should such a pair comport themselves in public? To touch or not to touch? Stand shoulder to shoulder or at arm's length? Handbag—yes or no? It was hard to predict what would look weird, offensive, ridiculous, or wrong.

And, all along, Ferraro had to field questions about whether—in the event she had to assume leadership of the country—she could be trusted to push the nuclear button, what with lady nerves and all. Also, did she ever cry at work? One Democratic politician asked in all sincerity, "Can you bake a blueberry muffin?"

Neither Ferraro's button-pushing nor her muffin-making ever did get road-tested. Mondale and Ferraro lost the '84 election in spectacular fashion, capturing just one state: Mondale's home, Minnesota. Maybe America wasn't ready for a mild-mannered middle-of-the-road white guy from the Midwest to become president. Oh wait, there'd already been a bunch of those. Maybe the nation just wasn't ready for a woman to ride shotgun.

THEN CAME 1985.

Right woman, right time, right place.

Wilma Pearl Mankiller. She was born November 18, 1945, in Tahlequah, Oklahoma, the sixth of eleven children. She was raised on Mankiller Flats, her Cherokee grandfather's land, where there was no running water or electricity; her clothes were sometimes made from flour sacks; and most of her family's food was obtained by hunting and fishing, growing and foraging. Extreme poverty might be an understatement. But she had her family around her, along with her family name. Mankiller. Potent and pointed. The name was a Cherokee military designation that had been in her family for generations. It was a stirring appellation for the first woman to become Principal Chief of the Cherokee Nation, but harder when she was, say, an eleven-year-old girl new to the rough streets of San Francisco, or a young single mother of two daughters trying to explain that her maiden name wasn't some feminist statement, but recovered history. Delightful or difficult, her name was also destiny.

Mankiller ended up in San Francisco after her family relocated from Oklahoma. The Indian Termination Policy had encouraged Natives to leave reservations and resettle in cities, where they were promised jobs and opportunity. Termination was a federal policy intended to do exactly what it sounds like: Make sovereign tribes extinct.

Termination was devised by Dillon Myer, the same upstanding asshat who'd organized the internment of Japanese Americans during World War II. Myer failed to consider (or it's what he had in mind) that cities come with zero guarantees, and that good jobs are always hard to get. Worse, in America's urban landscapes, Indians found themselves stranded, cut off from their cultures and people. In short, more than a hundred years after the Trail of Tears saw 4,000 Cherokee dead and 12,000 survivors relocated a thousand miles west of their homeland, Mankiller's family faced its own forced migration. She called it "My own little Trail of Tears."

Then came the Occupation of Alcatraz on November 20, 1969. Mankiller was more than a little uplifted when a group of some eighty Native men, women, and children calling themselves Indians of All Tribes (IAT) landed on the shuttered federal penitentiary in San Francisco Bay and commenced living there. Mankiller had a front-row seat to the grand spectacle—nineteen satisfying months of press briefings and protest. IAT cited the 1868 Treaty of Fort Laramie (between the United States government and the Sioux) that promised to return all abandoned federal lands to Natives. Alcatraz had been shut down in 1963 and declared "surplus federal property." Bam. So the occupiers did have a legal leg to stand on. They were not strictly Sioux, true, but they were "Indians of All Tribes." And when had the federal government ever been sticklers for treaties with Indians anyway?

One of the spokespeople for the IAT, Richard Oakes, issued the Alcatraz Proclamation and Letter to the San Francisco Department of the Interior. The full text is well worth reading. Among beautiful, terrible, satirical, and wise words, it kicks off with:

> We, the native Americans, re-claim the land known as Alcatraz Island in the name of all American Indians by right of discovery.
>
> We wish to be fair and honorable in our dealings with the Caucasian inhabitants of this land, and hereby offer the following treaty:
>
> We will purchase said Alcatraz Island for twenty-four ($24) in glass beads and red cloth, a precedent set by the white man's purchase of a similar island about 300 years ago.

You know how it ends, at least in a sense. Today Alcatraz is a tourist mecca run by the National Park Service, not a Native-run settlement with a university, health services, and cultural center, per the intentions of IAT. But the occupation was no failure. Many major federal policy and legal changes benefiting tribes happened as a result, including President Richard Nixon abolishing Termination.

But the biggest impact of the Occupation was less tangible than treaties, laws, and policies. It ignited passion, pride, and possibility. Mankiller's in particular.

★ ★ ★

As a teenager in San Francisco, she'd been ringside for the civil rights and women's rights movements. She'd lived around Black Panthers, especially admiring their dedication to feeding and educating children. She'd met community organizers like Dolores Huerta and Cesar Chavez. She'd seen women on the street protesting for their rights. But nothing lit a fire like the IAT.

The Occupation of Alcatraz changed everything. Transforming from housewife to activist almost overnight, Mankiller organized food and clothing donations for those on the island, and she visited when she could. "More than anything it felt like coming home," she said of her visits. "And I felt it was where I should be."

She tried to remain a dutiful wife, though her handsome Ecuadorean husband, who she'd married at age seventeen, did not approve of her un-housewifely activities. Nevertheless, she persisted. Mankiller was listening to other voices now.

She went back to school. First Skyline Community College, then San Francisco State, where so much activism was happening. Without telling her husband, she bought a car using money from their joint savings account. She wasn't asking for permission anymore. She started looking for where she could assist the Native community, from writing grant proposals to raising funds for legal defense. She stopped being shy. "My commitment to improving the lives of my own people was greater than my fear of speaking up in a meeting or making a fool of myself." She'd come to San Francisco a sheltered country girl thrown into public housing, never having used a flush toilet, never having been in an elevator,

and now she was someone other Natives relied on.

In 1974 Mankiller divorced her husband. As a single mother, she moved with her daughters to Oakland, where she was a social worker for the Urban Indian Resource Center, before deciding after a couple of years that it was time to go home. In 1971 she'd helped take her father's body back to Oklahoma for burial. That was home. She rented a U-Haul, packed up her teenage daughters and the family pets, and drove straight for Mankiller Flats.

The family home had been burned down by hunters, but the land was theirs, including a natural spring of fresh water. They made do.

Mankiller soon landed a modest position with the Cherokee government. Her small, typically thankless projects quickly started yielding big results. Famously, in the village of Bell, just fourteen miles from Mankiller flats, she encountered a community of three hundred Cherokee living without any modern amenities. She thought they needed a school, education being a ticket to better everything. But before putting any plan into practice, she asked the people of Bell what they wanted.

No one had ever asked them before. And so, defiantly or hopefully or cynically, the people in Bell said they wanted running water. Sure thing, Mankiller said, with no idea how she'd make it happen. She raised some money, but told the residents of Bell they'd need to handle everything else themselves, from digging ditches to laying pipe. Folks shook their heads, laughed, got pissed, yelled, stormed off. Many said it could never work.

Few thought it had any hope of success, from the residents of Bell to Cherokee leaders

to the Bureau of Indian Affairs itself. But Mankiller had seen what IAT had done at Alcatraz in just nineteen months, when a few Native bodies stood up to the entire federal government. She believed Bell's challenges were no more insurmountable. With the help of a Cherokee speaker and community activist named Charlie Soap (whom she'd later marry), she went house to house, community meeting after meeting, convincing residents of Bell that they could create a system for running water themselves. For a year mothers and grandmothers and children and young men and grandfathers moved earth, dug ditches by hand, and laid down sixteen miles of pipe. Self-sufficiency. Pride. Running water.

"I banked everything I believed on that project," Mankiller said. The tribe took notice.

In 1983, Principal Chief Ross Swimmer, a Republican, asked Mankiller, a Democrat, to join his ticket as Deputy Chief. No one much blinked at the blended political loyalties, but there was plenty of opposition to a woman as Deputy Chief of the Cherokee Nation (a job akin to Vice President of the United States, second-in-command of a sovereign nation). Mankiller squeaked to victory with 50.4 percent of the vote.

Two years later, in 1985, Ronald Reagan appointed Swimmer to a position in the federal government. Wilma Mankiller was now Principal Chief.

Historically important, a big deal, all of that—but *serving* as Chief isn't the same as being *elected* Chief. In 1987 Mankiller ran on her own ticket. The "overt sexism" she experienced was shocking, and dangerous. She received death threats, slashed car tires, gas-tank tampering, and other vandalism. Her image was burned in effigy. Many loudly and publicly insisted that electing a female chief would make the Cherokee a joke among tribes.

She won anyway. Her grit and ability to get things done spoke louder than gender. Laudatory articles in magazines like *People* and *Ms.* probably didn't hurt either. Mankiller was fast becoming nationally known as the face of the Cherokee people.

She won again in 1991, a landslide victory where she garnered 80 percent of the vote. Mankiller had by then become an internationally recognized leader, someone who had significantly grown the tribe from 55,000 to some 200,000 enrolled members, injected millions into the economy through grants and business initiatives, created new education opportunities from preschool through college, and spearheaded medical initiatives that led to the largest tribal healthcare system in the United States, staffed primarily by Cherokee doctors, dentists, nurses, and technicians.

Mankiller understood all too well the importance of good medical care. In 1979,

while she was driving one early morning to her job at tribal headquarters, an oncoming car passing on a blind curve hit her head on. She barely survived. The driver of the other car died at the scene. A double tragedy because this driver was Mankiller's best friend, Sherry Morris. Doctors told Mankiller she'd never walk again. It took seventeen operations, but she left the hospital on crutches. A kidney failed; one of her brothers donated his. Her other kidney went the same way; a niece donated one of hers. Mankiller also survived lymphoma and breast cancer. Then in 2010, she was diagnosed with pancreatic cancer.

By then Mankiller was a bestselling author, was the recipient of multiple honorary doctorates, and had been awarded the Presidential Medal of Freedom by President Bill Clinton. The night she died, indigenous leaders from twenty-three countries built bonfires high on mountaintops to usher her spirit safely home.

"In a just country," said her friend Gloria Steinem, "she would have been elected president."

CHAPTER 16

REPRESENT: GUERRILLA GIRLS

You know, wearing this mask gives you a certain kind of freedom to say whatever you want. I completely recommend it. If you're in a situation where you're a little afraid to speak up, put a mask on. You won't believe what comes out of your mouth.

GUERRILLA GIRL "FRIDA KAHLO"

YOU GUYS, the eighties were totally rad! So many killer firsts, right? Including—but definitely not limited to—Wilma Mankiller. Women had arrived.

Right?

Not so fast. From defeat of the Equal Rights Amendment in 1982, to the bombing of abortion clinics, to a notorious 1986 *Newsweek* cover story with statistics designed to scare the crap out of "career women," plenty of backlash came concurrent with gains.

The infamous *Newsweek* story—"Too Late for Prince Charming?"—included so-called statistics informing women interested in marriage that "Forty-year-olds are more likely to be killed by a terrorist: They have a minuscule 2.6 percent probability of tying the knot."

It turned out *Newsweek*'s stats were incorrect. But the stress they provoked was real. And that, really, was the whole point. The three-thousand-word article, with the names of six reporters attached—all of it telegraphing serious journalism—was a bony index finger pointed straight at women's choices.

Hey babes, you made your beds so lie in 'em. And cry.

Of course, not all women wanted to get married (or to men). But many did, or at least wanted the option. And they were told: No, you can't have it all. It's feminism or your life.

Two steps forward, two steps back. Maybe three.

Imagine some four years before that *Newsweek* issue landed: You'd laced up your white Reebok tennies, donned your best business suit with the silk lady tie, and marched for the Equal Rights Amendment—the one that Congress had been kicking down the road since 1921 (though it's recently back from the dead, so maybe still kicking), the amendment that would legally establish that men and women are equal in all things, like oh, say, equal pay for equal work. Maybe at that ERA march you felt connected to suffragists of yore, ready to keep up the fight for as long as it took. Then you headed over to work and kicked ass in your career.

And then this brutal *Newsweek* issue left you feeling deflated and hopeless.

The magazine eventually disavowed the article and its numbers—like, twenty years later. But by then the psychic damage was done. As the *New York Times* wrote, "For a lot of women, the retraction doesn't matter. The article seems to have lodged itself permanently in the national psyche."

★ ★ ★

WHILE MAINSTREAM MEDIA brandished flawed stats to target feminism, women artists in New York had already seized on statistics to make their own point: Women were nowhere near equality. And it wasn't their fault.

In 1984, the Museum of Modern Art issued a press release for their major *International*

Survey of Contemporary Art, a show intended to "reveal the high quality and extraordinary vitality of recent artistic production." The show featured 195 works, from seventeen countries. Getting selected for this survey was a BFD. Curator Kynaston McShine (yes, real name) went so far as to say that any artist who didn't get invited needed to reevaluate *his* career. He did not misspeak. Of the show's 182 artists, only thirteen were women, all of them white. Well.

Soon after, seven women artists met in a SoHo loft to plot their collective response. "We didn't have a plan," one said years later. "We were just pissed off." They named a secretary and began scripting one. They weren't the types to sit around waiting twenty years for a retraction.

They decided to steal a page from artists like Faith Ringgold, co-founder of the Ad Hoc Women Artists' Committee (Ad Hoc). Fifteen years earlier, she had targeted the Whitney Museum of American Art, demanding that women receive 50 percent representation in the Whitney's upcoming *Painting and Sculpture Annual* (what became its *Biennial*), and that all exhibitions "reflect the ethnic distribution of the metropolitan area in which the show is being given." Ringgold and cohorts relied on guerrilla tactics like fake press releases, forged press passes, and museum infiltrators who booby-trapped (see what I did there?) galleries with female iconography like, oh, say, eggs and sanitary napkins. Stats backed up the effectiveness of such actions. The 1969 Whitney *Painting Biennial* came in with less than 5 percent women, while its 1970 *Sculpture Biennial* was up to 22 percent. Hardly parity and yet a huge improvement.

Ad Hoc's actions, alongside Linda Nochlin's "Why Are There No Great Women Artists?" which landed around the same time (see chapter 12), should have been a one-two punch to patriarchal art practices. But by the mid-eighties, the art world had already forgotten the lessons of the recent past.

The women artists stewing in that SoHo loft in early '85 were not pleased. Inspired by Ad Hoc and others, they decided to go full guerrilla, embracing the word in full. To quote *Merriam-Webster*, "irregular military actions (such as harassment and sabotage) carried out by small usually independent forces." Ideal. And since guerrillas regularly hide their features, the women needn't fear art world reprisals. To be anonymous was to be bold. Everyone liked the idea.

The secretary transcribing the SoHo meeting scribbled furiously to keep up with ideas ricocheting around the room. In her haste, she made a felicitous mistake, writing "gorilla" for "guerrilla." Spelling error as stroke of genius. Gorilla masks were funny and weird, especially when paired with skirts and heels. Gorillas were also big and hairy and angry-looking. A little threatening. Yes, this would be the group's disguise. It ticked so many excellent boxes. For example, in the way motherhood had been wielded against suffragists, humorlessness was brandished against feminists in the seventies and eighties. Enter the Guerrilla Girls, with hairy heads and spike heels, fierce satire backed up by hard cold statistics.

Gorilla masks on, the original seven women (who would grow to over a hundred anonymous members) started by pointing fingers and naming names.

Their first action went up in April 1985, with posters plastered all over SoHo spelling things out in stark black and white: WHAT DO THESE ARTISTS HAVE IN COMMON? followed by the names of dozens of successful male artists listed in alphabetical order, then: THEY ALLOW THEIR WORK TO BE SHOWN IN GALLERIES THAT SHOW NO MORE THAN 10% WOMEN ARTISTS OR NONE AT ALL. It was signed, GUERILLA GIRLS, CONSCIENCE OF THE ART WORLD.

More broadsides followed. Galleries that showed no women (or not enough) appeared on the posters. So did art critics who didn't give enough column inches to women.

The Guerrilla Girls started giving interviews and press conferences. Wearing gorilla heads (also pearls, miniskirts, etc.) made them difficult to differentiate, so they went by code names, all of which paid homage to women artists who came before them. Elizabeth Vigée-Lebrun and Rosalba Carriera of the eighteenth century; Frida Kahlo and Käthe Kollwitz of the twentieth. By naming their foremothers, the Guerrilla Girls reinserted women artists of the past—often forgotten or overlooked or undervalued—into the current art world.

One of the Guerrilla Girls' greatest hits was a poster titled THE ADVANTAGES OF BEING A WOMAN ARTIST. The thirteen "advantages" that followed included, "Working without the pressure of success," and "Knowing your career might pick up after you're eighty." And my favorite, "Not having to undergo the embarrassment of being called a genius."

In 1989 a group of Guerrilla Girls infiltrated the Metropolitan Museum of Art with clipboards to conduct a "wienie count" of the massive collection. The result is their most iconic and arresting poster. One might even call it feminist graffiti. Done in the long landscape style of a bus advertisement, it shows French (male) painter Jean-Auguste-Dominique Ingres's famous painting, *La Grande Odalisque*—a come-hither Orientalized nude—surmounted by a snarling gorilla head. The caption reads in bold: "Do women have to be naked to get into the Met. Museum?" And, just below that gem: "Less than 5% of the artists in the Modern Art Sections are women, but 85% of the nudes are female."

Maybe the saddest part about that statistic is that it's not terribly surprising. But it annoyed the art world. Few liked that the Guerrillas were dealing in impossible-to-ignore facts.

★ ★ ★

THOSE FACTS PERSIST. In 2012 the Guerrilla Girls went back to the Met, then recreated their Ingres odalisque poster with new stats: "Do women have to be naked to get into the Met. Museum?" was still there in big bold letters. The change was below: "Less than 4% of the artists in the Modern Art Sections are women, but 76% of the nudes are female."

That's right, in 2012 there were in fact fewer women artists in America's premier museum than in the 1980s. But more naked men.

THE YEAR OF THE WOMAN

1992

CHAPTER 17

YEAR OF THE WOMAN

The Statue of Freedom, the Statue of Liberty, these are icons, not real women that girls and women can look up to. We want real women, not icons.

KAREN STASER, WOMAN SUFFRAGE STATUE CAMPAIGN

EVERYONE LIKES TO REMIND ME THAT I DID NOT WIN. I LIKE TO SAY I WON, BECAUSE I SHARED MY STORY.

ANITA HILL

IT WAS LIVE TELEVISION. Anything could happen. There she stood, right hand raised, taking the oath saying she would tell the whole truth. Nothing but the truth. Like millions of other people glued to televisions across the country, I could not look away.

It was easy to see she didn't want to be there, with cameras recording her from every angle and a bank of senators staring down at her. She had some difficult things to relay about the Supreme Court nominee. Sexual and coercive and, one would assume, extremely damaging things. She chose her words with careful deliberation.

None of it seemed to matter. Because nearly thirty years later, I sat glued to a different screen, watching a different woman professor make similar claims about another Supreme Court nominee in front of a familiar panel of senators.

In both cases, the nominee was approved, and his eloquent female accuser called a liar, then publicly shamed.

Anita Hill: Clarence Thomas. 1991.

Christine Blasey Ford: Brett Kavanaugh. 2018.

History repeating itself—in one lifetime. Enraging.

I shouldn't claim the events are totally indistinguishable. Hill was scolded by the senators there to hear her story, accused of erotomania (a theory asking us to believe she was hot for Thomas and made it all up), and described by journalist David Brock as "a little bit nutty and a little bit slutty." Blasey Ford, in her turn, was relentlessly mocked (including by the President of the United States) and memed (shared by at least one Republican congressman), and months after her testimony still can't return to her job or go home with her family out of fear of violence (by which I mean murder). Public shaming may have changed some, but a familiar viciousness remains.

Meanwhile, Clarence Thomas and Brett Kavanaugh assumed lifetime appointments to the United States Supreme Court, a position wherein nine Americans are entrusted to sit in judgment of some 330 million more.

Why, it's enough to make you . . . vote.

On the heels of the Thomas mess (and on the heels of Kavanaugh, too), women came out in droves to elect their own kind. In 1992, twenty-four women were elected to the House (for a total of forty-seven, up from twenty-eight) and four to the Senate (for a grand total of six). Huzzah! Of the 535 congressional and senate positions in the Capitol, women held 53. Nearly a solid 10 percent. The Year of the Woman!

Perhaps you, like me, do not find these numbers all that thrilling. Perhaps you, like me, might be aware that there was still only one woman on the Supreme Court and there'd not yet been a female secretary of state, much less vice president or president. One seasoned legislator, Senator Barbara Mikulski (Democrat, Maryland), spoke with particular sharpness on the subject of mislaid celebration: "Calling 1992 the Year of the Woman makes it sound like the Year of the Caribou or the Year of the Asparagus," she said. "We're not a fad, a fancy, or a year." Mikulski knew what she was talking about. She'd been legislating since 1977 and would still be there three decades later when her colleague Hillary Clinton lost the election that would have made her the first female president.

But let's not allow the bigger challenges to erase the significant gains of that year. Women were elected in historic numbers. One of them, the junior senator from Illinois, Carol Moseley Braun, fit a similar description to Anita Hill. Law school, ambitious, black. You might argue that Moseley Braun was a Midwest poke in Clarence Thomas's eye.

In twenty years Moseley Braun went from University of Chicago Law grad to state rep to U.S. senator. Known for her easy smile and iron-willed optimism, she embodied all kinds of badassery: first African American Democrat in the Senate; first African American woman in the Senate; only African American senator during her entire term; one of only two African American senators in the entire twentieth century; first woman to wear pants in the Senate chamber. Oh yep, you read that last one right.

★ ★ ★

IT WAS A COLD D.C. MORNING in January 1993, shortly after her election, and Moseley Braun knew just the thing for it. Raised in Chicago, she was hardly a stranger to inclement weather, and she'd seen more than her share in a decade serving in the Illinois legislature. In her closet she quickly selected a favorite suit, her "nice outfit," one she'd often worn in Springfield. She headed into work, her mind already buzzing with morning tasks—personnel, pending legislation, interviews—ready to tackle every angle of her new job. What she wasn't prepared for was

fashion-shaming. But that's what she got. The "gasps were audible," she later recounted. Her fellow senators, 94 percent men, knew what she did not: Pants were forbidden in the Senate.

Well, pants on women.

"It was one of those unwritten rules that they don't tell you about unless you're part of the circle," Moseley Braun said years later. "And nobody was talking to me about these things so I had no clue." Fashion policing fell to the Capitol Doorkeeper, a real job by the way, with real power to stop anyone from coming inside, senator to Senate page. But since the "no pants" rule was an unwritten one, Moseley Braun moseyed her way into the Senate chamber. Where social opprobrium from fellow senators was apparent, but where they couldn't do much more than frown, shake heads, and stare daggers.

Her party-foul reception astonished Moseley Braun and it ticked off her female colleague Senator Mikulski (of "Year of The Caribou" fame). Mikulski had been itching to wear trousers to work forever, so that winter she did. Unlike Braun, Mikulski knew what she was setting herself up for. "You would have thought that I was walking on the moon," she said of the reaction that followed.

Newspapers may have been quick to treat the appearance of pants on women senators like something from outer space, but women journalists covering the Senate seized the opportunity to don slacks, and so did female staffers. Moseley Braun dubbed it "the pantsuit revolution."

Fortunately, pants weren't the only victory for women in the legislature in the wake of

The Year of the Woman. Would significant laws like the Family and Medical Leave Act and the Violence Against Women Act have passed without the influx of women legislators? Unlikely. Indignities born of the Anita Hill hearings had been turned into clear political power.

Male senators held tight to what gender perks they could. If you think women not being allowed to wear pants until 1993 is crazy, it wasn't until 2009 that women were allowed to swim in the Senate pool. Apparently some boy senators liked to swim sans skivvies and didn't want girl senators peeking at their privates. So, No Girls Allowed!

To paraphrase that classic Guerrilla Girls poster: Do you have to be naked (and male) to get into the Senate swimming pool?

★ ★ ★

PETTY POOL RULES ASIDE, the bulldozer that was The Year of the Woman wasn't done with leveling the playing field yet.

Next up: The *Portrait Monument*.

Remember the seven-ton sculpture from the introduction, the one carved by artist and suffragist Adelaide Johnson, completed in 1921? The one depicting Lucretia Mott, Elizabeth Cady Stanton, and Susan B. Anthony alongside a looming fourth chunk of uncarved stone, all of them rising from a massive block of rough Carrara marble?

If you've forgotten, count yourself average. So had everyone else in 1995.

After a grand pageant dedicating the *Portrait Monument* to Congress in 1921, the massive artwork was consigned to the Capitol Crypt (a kind of elegant basement), like, the very next day. And, its offending feminist inscription in gold was then chipped off by an official act of Congress.

Believe it or not, it wasn't clear at first that going to the crypt was a bad thing. It was originally built to hold the remains of George Washington (it never did), and the Architect of the Capitol had recently suggested that much of the building's statuary go on display there. But it didn't happen that way, and soon the crypt was being used as a kind of service closet, filled with mops and brooms and cleaning supplies, and a big chunk of sculpted marble. The founding mothers of women's suffrage deserved better.

In 1995, a future founder of the National Women's History Museum, Karen Staser, was visiting the crypt— in 1963 it had been spruced up and made available to the public, including a nice souvenir counter—and noticed the sculpture nearby. She had no idea what she was looking at exactly, or who, besides Susan B. Anthony, was depicted. There was no wall label, but something about it struck her as memorable. Maybe the unusual sight of three women commemorated in stone. Later that day, her hunch was confirmed when, visiting a local suffrage site, she saw a poster with the *Portrait Monument* on it and realized what she'd stumbled upon *in the crypt*.

She was on the lookout for women's stories, and this was a blockbuster. There was no way the Portrait Monument could remain hidden underground.

Staser enlisted her husband, a staffer for Alaska senator Ted Stevens (R), to help. Stevens, it turned out, had been raised by suffragists and was happy to come onboard. In short order, the Senate unanimously approved the sculpture's relocation. But the House was another story. The House Speaker at the time was a guy named Newt Gingrich, who resembled his name in that he was apparently cold-blooded. Gingrich polled the women in his caucus and a handful voted against relocating the sculpture. Done deal; the House majority would oppose any move.

Undaunted, Staser called Gingrich and schooled him on the history of the women of the *Portrait Monument*, including their political inclinations, telling him, "So, you have locked three Republican women in the basement." Negotiations began in earnest. Gingrich wouldn't allow any funds he oversaw—public or private—to be spent on relocating the sculpture, which was estimated to cost $75,000 (despite, just a few years before, the Capitol Preservation Commission spending $750,000 to conserve the *Statue of Freedom*, the allegorical female figure atop the Capitol dome). So money had to be raised separately, from private sources.

But there was still the problem of the artwork itself. Many legislators, including several female ones, felt it was unattractive, and not worthy of bringing aboveground. To complaints about the *Portrait Monument*'s lack of elegance, I say take a walk around the Capitol and you'll get an eyeful of regrettable artwork. So what? It's not an art museum, it's a repository for the elevation and contemplation of our shared history. And as Congresswoman Pat Schroeder put it at the time of the debate: "Have you looked at Abraham Lincoln lately?" and "The whole place is filled with statues where the cuteness issue never came up."

I will grant you that the *Portrait Monument* is off-putting: the busts of three women half liberated from a marble slab but still imprisoned in it—you can almost sense their poor pinned-down arms and the rest of their bodies still trapped in stone. Maybe Johnson's way of conveying that all those women had was their voices, together and separately.

So, as public sculpture it's a little odd. But stranger than, say, Rodin's *Monument to Balzac* in Paris? Not so much. Also, as noted art historian and critic Aruna D'Souza once tweeted, "Effigies of famous individuals are a really freaking stupid way to commemorate history, period." (Word.)

But if we are going to create likenesses of historically important figures, then women need to be included. In the days when lawmakers were cooking up plans to move the *Monument*, the Rotunda saw four million visitors a year. There, the only image depicting a real woman was a mural titled *The Baptism of Pocahontas*. Personally, I'm not so into romanticizing in a significant American governmental institution the religious conversion of a Native teenager while she was being held hostage by English settlers. But maybe that's just me.

Regardless: one woman; so many men.

★ ★ ★

NONE OF THE AESTHETIC OBJECTIONS

to the *Portrait Monument* held water. What's more, according to one of the women spearheading the move, "This statue was the one the suffragists gave us. This statue is the one through which all women in America

were dishonored when it was shoved in the basement." Fair enough.

Funds were raised. Moving was arranged.

And then opposition from an unexpected but understandable quarter: African American women, citing the obvious exclusion of any black women in this vision of the "mothers" of women's suffrage. This was nearly the fatal blow.

Why not, these women suggested, carve Sojourner Truth into that fourth section of marble? It's a pretty elegant solution. Perhaps a missed opportunity. But among other objections—Who? How?—Moseley Braun, the Senate's sole African American legislator, felt they needed to press on. Four previous attempts to move the work over seven decades had gone down in flames. She thought it better to relocate the *Portrait Monument* as it was— and create a separate monument to Truth.

In the end that's what happened, and as fate would have it the bronze bust of Sojourner Truth would be dedicated in the Capitol by America's first black first lady, Michelle Obama.

★ ★ ★

THE *MONUMENT* HAD BEEN DEDICATED

on February 15, 1921, a mere six months after the ratification of the Nineteenth Amendment, in a pageant that included abundant flowers, rented capes, multiple descendants of famous suffragists, verbose banners declaring women's rights and history, a full chorus, and the U.S. Marine Band at the Capitol, all on the 101st birthday of Susan B. Anthony.

In dedicating the work, activist Sara Bard Field declared: "Mr. Speaker, you will see that if you thought you came here tonight to receive on behalf of Congress merely the busts of three women who have fought the good fight and gone to rest, you were mistaken. You will see that through them it is the body and the blood of a great sacrificial host which we present— the body and the blood of Revolution, the body and blood of Freedom herself."

Yeek. Quite the overtly religious metaphor for a secular monument.

And yet.

On an overcast and rainy Sunday three-quarters of a century later, Mother's Day 1997, women who'd advocated for relocation of the *Portrait Monument* watched for a second day as workmen struggled to raise seven tons of stone from one floor to another. With so much stone and marble, it was cold inside and out. And deflating, too, as the move was taking so much longer than anticipated.

But then, finally, the workmen had it. And just as the statue entered the Rotunda at long last, the rain stopped and a beam of light broke through the dark sky like the hand of God in a Baroque painting. Cue heavenly music. Cue tears. Into the light.

CHAPTER 18

THIRD WAVE: RIOT GRRRL

BECAUSE I believe with my whole-heartmindbody that girls constitute a revolutionary soul force that can, and will change the world for real.

KATHLEEN HANNA, BIKINI KILL ZINE NO. 2

WOMEN ARE NATURAL ANARCHISTS.

KIM GORDON, SONIC YOUTH

YOU KNOW WHAT ELSE WAS HAPPENING in Washington, D.C., in the early nineties? Riot Grrrl was making the scene (and making a scene). Some punk rockers from Olympia, Washington, relocated to D.C. to hang with girl punks there. Together they started a new zine called *Riot Grrrl*. They had not come to play nice. Grrr.

One of them, twenty-two year-old Kathleen Hanna, soon to be reluctant figurehead of the Riot Grrrl movement, had started a band the year before with a crystal clear feminist agenda. Her band, Bikini Kill, also had an eponymous zine, in the second issue of which they published a *Riot Grrrl Manifesto*, written by Hanna. Though the xeroxed, hand-stapled zine was likely seen by just a few hundred people at most, it's a document whose fierce flame still burns bright—and throws shade—today. Ever hear that Brian Eno comment

about how "the first Velvet Underground album only sold 10,000 copies, but everyone who bought it formed a band"? The *Riot Grrrl Manifesto* was like that. It punched way above its weight class.

I picture those punk rock girls like late-twentieth-century versions of Elizabeth Cady Stanton and Lucretia Mott, sitting around Mary Ann M'Clintock's mahogany table, sipping sugarless tea while Cady Stanton's quill furiously scratched away. But these grrrls were wearing kilts and combat boots, with scissors and glue at the ready, while Hanna hunched over a typewriter.

The Manifesto declared sixteen points, beginning with:

BECAUSE us girls crave records and books and fanzines that speak to US that WE feel included in and can understand in our own ways. *Onward to*, BECAUSE we are unwilling to falter under claims that we are reactionary "reverse sexists" AND NOT THE TRUEPUNKROCKSOULCRUSADERS THAT WE KNOW we really are, and BECAUSE we are angry at a society that tells us Girl = Dumb, Girl = Bad, Girl = Weak.

And so it went in awesome, fearsome fashion.

Riot Grrrl was a community of bands, zines, consciousness-raising, and sartorial statements that included skirts, boots, sassy haircuts, and exposed skin used as signage. Wielding pithy phrases like weapons—Riots Not Diets; Riot = Not Quiet; Girls to the Front—Riot Grrl was a maelstrom of bellies, breasts, blistering lyrics, feedback, and feminist rage. It was beautiful to behold.

Riot Grrrl insisted on a somehow revolutionary concept: *Girls rock too.* What's more, they had something important to say—so sit down, shut up, and listen.

This did not go over well, not with a lot of dudes in the punk scene, not with "beergut-boyrock" (to quote the *Manifesto*) bastions of power in the mainstream music industry, and not with some second-wave feminists.

Shall we take those one by one?

Punk rock boys: Their zines printed assessments of Riot Grrrl bands like Bikini Kill, Bratmobile, and Team Dresch with thoughtful observations like "bitches," "man-haters" and "dykes." All of these were reclaimed by Riot Grrrl via lipstick or Sharpie across, say, a bare expanse of stomach, breast, or upper thigh. All the same, it wasn't easy. "It was also super schizo," Hanna wrote, "to play shows where guys threw stuff at us, called us cunts, and yelled 'take it off' during our set, and then the next night perform for throngs of amazing girls singing along to every lyric and cheering after every song."

Mainstream "beergutboyrock": In addition to many national mags writing off Riot Grrrl wholesale, *Rolling Stone* eviscerated Bikini Kill's first album, *Revolution Girl Style Now!* as "yowling and moronic nag-unto-vomit tantrums." (Worth saying, it's an ass-kicking album you should download immediately. I'm so jealous of generations after mine. When I was young we had to walk through snow uphill both ways to the record store and then—they wouldn't have the album! When that happened, you had to mail order it by *writing a letter* and enclosing money. There you go: history lesson.)

While we're on *Rolling Stone*, as I write this, it has just been announced an upcoming show at the Metropolitan Museum of Art (where I was employed during the Riot Grrrl years; when upon occasion I saw bands like Bratmobile, Huggy Bear, and Bikini Kill downtown after work and on weekends). Called *Play It Loud: Instruments of Rock & Roll,* the Met show is a secular display of relics—i.e., guitars—from the holy order of rock gods (1939–2017). And I do mean gods: Jimi Hendrix, Eric Clapton, Eddie Van Halen, Jerry Garcia, Pete Townsend . . . the list in *Rolling Stone* goes on like that. There's just one Hail Mary—i.e., woman—in the bunch, the coincidentally religious-sounding St. Vincent. Out of 130 instruments from "seventy public and private collections" mentioned in the magazine, there's just one belonging to a woman, a far worse percentage than the Met count that gave birth to the Guerrilla Girls.

Since I'm slagging on *Rolling Stone*, in a recent exchange with online art magazine *Hyperallergic*, they claim Alice Cooper should count toward the pitifully small number of women they've featured on their covers. No, not sculptor Alice Cooper who made the heroic Sacajawea bronze in Portland, but the rocker (and all male) Alice Cooper who fronted a band of the same name while wearing makeup and the occasional dress.

This is what Riot Grrrl was up against. What women are still up against.

Second-wave feminists: Older women were flummoxed by the embrace of a word like "girl" when they'd fought so hard to be called women (not *babe, chick, girl, Miss, Mrs.,* etc.). They disapproved, even if *girl* was spelled with

a growl in it. Many were further concerned by said "girls" wearing crop tops with "slut" or "bitch" or even "cunt" scrawled across their bellies, while sporting pigtails, pink barrettes, and baby doll T-shirts. Second-wave feminists had—understandably—insisted: *I am not a sex object and my body is not up for scrutiny by the male gaze.* Riot Grrrl said: *These tits, this ass, are mine to do with as I will and fuck off male gaze 'cause I know you're looking.*

Sex-positive and public about it, Riot Grrrl was also volubly anti–rape culture and anti-objectification, a paradoxical stance that second-wave feminists found problematic. For many feminists of the previous generation, wearing baby doll T-shirts and short skirts was the precise opposite of a feminist act. But what older feminists saw as capitulation to male desire, Riot Grrrl saw as claiming their own bodies. And unlike earlier feminists, Riot Girrl was a lot less concerned with legislative gains for women than with burning that shit down. They were explicitly anti-capitalist. They did not see achieving the corner office as winning anything.

Riot Grrrl is sometimes credited with giving life to so-called "third wave" feminism, but it's fairer to say that the wave was a timely force of nature and they were poised to ride it. The phrase itself was coined by Rebecca Walker in a 1992 *Ms.* article in direct response to Anita Hill's wrenching, disregarded testimony. In "Becoming the Third Wave," Walker could not have been clearer, "So I write this as a plea to all women, especially women of my generation: Let Thomas's confirmation serve to remind you, as it did me, that the fight is far from over. Let this dismissal of a woman's

experience move you to anger. Turn that outrage into political power." It concluded, "I am not a post-feminism feminist. I am the Third Wave."

Rebecca Walker is the daughter of influential second-wave feminist, author, and onetime *Ms.* editor, Alice Walker. And her assertive article proved the perfect illustration of one generation pushing against another. *Thank you, now I'll do it myself.*

One thing third-wave feminism explicitly embraced was intersectionality, recognizing the different layers of discrimination women face: gender of course but also race, sexuality, size, class, mobility, etc. Things that feminism's first and second waves had hardly recognized, or had explicitly denied (though second-wave feminists like Alice Walker had certainly tried to wake white women up).

That said, Riot Grrrl was pretty damn white, and even within a community promoting diversity, there was friction. You can see it in the trove of art and zines left in its wake, like Ramdasha Bikceem's *GUNK*, which described the many ways her white punk rock peers didn't get it, and *Bamboo Girl*, by Sabrina Margarita Alcantara-Tan, among many others. Zine creator (*Slant, Slander, Race Riot*) and academic Mimi Thi Nguyen has said these zines were needed to reject the depiction within Riot Grrrl of women of color as "voiceless victims or objects-to-be-rescued of white punk anti-racist discourses."

★ ★ ★

AND YET IT'S BIKINI KILL'S Kathleen Hanna who still endures as the face of Riot Grrrl. But

in 2012, she told the *New Yorker* that whenever women ask how they can reawaken the Riot Grrrl movement, she tells them, "Don't revive it, make something better."

That's been happening all along. In late-nineties New York, hardcore musician Tamar-kali Brown felt isolated in the scene until she met fellow Afropunks Maya Glick and Simi Stone, who both played in bands. They created their own scene in the East Village, including Sista Grrrls Riot, showcasing black women in bands. There are stories like this all over the world. Including some internationally known punk rock activists in Russia who've been making news with an English name: Pussy Riot.

Riot Grrrls Not Dead.

CHAPTER 19

YOUNG AMERICANS

I believe that every woman's soul is haunted by the spirits of earlier women who fought for their unmet needs and those of their children and their tribes and their peoples . . . who took risks and resisted.

ADRIENNE RICH, SMITH COLLEGE COMMENCEMENT, 1979

My friends and I might still be eleven, and we might still be in elementary school, but we know. We know life isn't equal for everyone and we know what's right and wrong. . . . And we know that we have seven short years until we, too, have the right to vote.

NAOMI WADLER, MARCH FOR OUR LIVES, WASHINGTON, D.C., 2018

OPEN LETTER to my daughter, age seventeen:

Forgive me this public missive. I appreciate your tolerance, here and always. What I want to tell you is this: I admire you more than I can say. You and so many young women who stand in their truth and speak up. I can only pray that we listen.

★ ★ ★

I write this less than a month after the 2018 midterm elections, with thirty-five new women coming into Congress, joining seventy already there. At long last there'll be over one hundred women in the House of Representatives. Hardly parity, but a great milestone. Also pretty great: the women them-selves. This incoming class of representatives includes Debra Haaland and Sharice Davids, the first Native women elected to Congress (with Davids just the third open lesbian), also the first Muslim women, Rashida Tlaib and Ilhan Omar, and the youngest woman ever elected to Congress, Alexandria Ocasio-Cortez. There were many other firsts for women in specific states. All this is, it seems to me, a heartening step in the right direction. Which is to say, a diversity of voices, the true fruits of universal suffrage.

And even so, it's hard to be a mother in America right now. Difficult to look at my children, particularly my teenage daughter, and not feel afraid. But here's what makes me feel a little less so: you.

For one thing, you're already leading. When I was your age, I wasn't hip to positive action. I was mostly just pissed off, wanting Reagan out and Doc Martens on. They were somewhat equivalent desires. I called myself a feminist, but it was a personal, inchoate kind of feminism. I looked for women in history, and in art and music and books, for inspiration. In hopes that their lives and work would reveal a map I could somehow follow. I did not stop to think how I might help others. But you do. Much of your generation does.

We saw it after the mass murder at Marjory Stoneman Douglas High School in Parkland, Florida. It was every parent's worst nightmare. Send your children off to school and they do not come home again. I watched the aftermath on TV and felt the same helpless anger I'd felt nearly twenty years before, watching the Columbine massacre unfold on live television, holding your brother, not even a year old, tightly in my arms.

But this time was different. Three days after the Parkland shooting, an eighteen-year-old named Emma González called BS on all of it. I'm being literal here, as I'm sure you know. González was part of a televised rally in front of the Broward County Courthouse, a gathering of survivors speaking out against guns and the pathetic state of gun control. "I knew I would get my job done properly at that rally if I got people chanting something. And I thought 'We call BS' has four syllables, that's good, I'll use that." That's what she told Ellen DeGeneres, afterward. *We call BS!* She'd chosen those words with deceptive care, already thinking like a savvy orator, or poet. She reminded me of you. Strong and smart and eloquent.

★ ★ ★

AFTER THEIR PROTEST at the Broward County Courthouse, González and fellow survivors called for a show of hands against guns. The country responded.

I know you walked out of school with your classmates (I spotted you on your school's Instagram), as part of #NeverAgain, the gun control movement started by those Marjory Stoneman Douglas students. I was at another high school to give a talk about writing and art. When I'd pulled up, hundreds of students were gathered on the school football field, making speeches. Later they would give me an orange wrist band they'd made to wear in protest and commemoration. It blows me away that you're surrounded by teenagers like this. I'm so grateful.

Even in states where guns are sacrosanct, there were protests, and almost always spearheaded by young people. And I mean young. In Virginia, an eleven-year-old girl named Naomi Wadler woke up to news that the daughter of a friend of her mom's had been shot in the back at Marjory Stoneman Douglas and didn't make it. She heard about the high school students' plan and thought, *I want to do a walkout, too.* In science class she asked Carter Anderson, her friend since kindergarten, if he'd join her. On the same day you walked out, Naomi and Carter stood with sixty-some grade schoolers on the lawn outside their school. Naomi held a blue sign above her head nearly as big as she was. Her message filled every inch: *#NeverAgain*. Beside her, Carter's sign was orange: *I will remember Courtlin Arrington #neveragain.*

Courtlin Arrington was the same age you are now, seventeen. She had not been killed at Marjory Stoneman Douglas on Valentine's Day, but at her Alabama high school three weeks

later. Her death had not received national attention. But while students across America stood silent for seventeen minutes to honor the dead of Parkland, Florida, the grade school kids on the lawn in Virginia stood in silence for eighteen. They added a minute for Arrington.

How could they be so wise, and so willing?

I'm guessing they knew about the political power of hashtags from activists they'd heard about their whole lives. Like Patrisse Cullors, Alicia Garza, and Opal Tometi, three young women who created a nationwide crusade called #BlackLivesMatter in 2013, demanding justice and safety for African Americans. Or a woman named Tarana Burke who, back in 2006, started using the phrase Me Too on Myspace (have you or your friends even heard of Myspace?) to make clear how many women have experienced sexual assault. In 2017 her #MeToo became shorthand for a social tsunami.

#NeverAgain kept going as well. Ten days after the walkouts, student organizers orchestrated more than 880 March for Our Lives protests across the country. Together, they constituted one of the largest organized multicity protests in American history. In Washington, D.C., survivors from Marjory Stoneman Douglas High spoke before a crowd of more than a quarter of a million people. Before many millions if you include those watching on television and online, as I was.

Emma González was one of the speakers in Washington. I held it together at first, even at the stricken sight of her relaying things her fallen classmates would never do again—wave, tease, play basketball, complain about practicing piano. Did you see her speech? I'm guessing you did, though we haven't talked about it. The way she just stood there, silent, minute after long minute, until six minutes and twenty seconds had passed—the length of time it took one gunman to take seventeen lives. I lost it. I'd never seen anything so moving, or so brave.

That is until eleven-year-old Naomi Wadler took the stage and said, with preternatural poise, "I am here to acknowledge the African American girls whose stories do not make the front pages of every national newspaper, whose stories don't lead on the evening news." The crowd erupted. The internet did too, with calls for one or both of them to run for president. Kamala Harris, just the second African American woman ever elected to the U.S. Senate, shared a clip of Wadler's speech. González was soon the face on artworks of a kind usually reserved for legends like Dolores Huerta or Che Guevara.

I can't help but imagine Lucretia Mott and Sojourner Truth, those giants of nineteenth-century oratory, casting their eyes across two centuries to the stirring sight of Emma and Naomi there onstage in the nation's capital, and smiling at their awesomeness. No doubt shocked by their hairstyles, not to mention pants, but so proud.

★ ★ ★

Another reason I have hope: In less than a year, you'll be eligible to vote. A year after that you'll cast your vote for president of the United States. Who knows what all you'll accomplish.

No pressure. You don't have to get onstage in front of millions of people. You do you, and change will come.

It will. I sometimes think about the nuclear missile silos once arrayed across the plains surrounding my hometown. When I was in middle school, a teacher told us we'd all burn to ash if those missiles ever launched, and everyone assumed they would eventually. I am here to tell you that Great Falls, Montana, is still there and many of those silos have been filled with gravel and sealed with cement. It can happen like that.

There are victories like those, yes, but also losses. As I write this, eighty-six Californians not so far from us have died in wildfires related to climate change.

I know you want to fight fires. When I was your age I didn't realize women could become firefighters. But there's no reason why you won't do it and I have every faith you will. Of course, the thought scares me, but you know what scares me more? That you could be prevented from pursuing your dream simply because of your gender.

We have the twin luxuries of knowing that you are entirely capable and that the door is open for you to walk through. Brave women before you kicked that door open. You have choices—innumerable choices—thanks to the women in the chapters preceding this one, their hard work and sacrifice.

★ ★ ★

I'LL CLOSE WITH THE POETS. First, Mojave language activist Natalie Diaz. Remember her? She stayed at our house one spring when you were eleven. I'm guessing you were as impressed by her basketball CV—NCAA Final Four, pro ball abroad—as by the poetry part. I doubt she'd mind. Natalie inspired me to read more poetry, especially by Native women—Joy Harjo, Heid Erdrich, Layli Long Soldier—and woke me up to current Native activism. Like those missile silos, the injustices done to Native communities surrounded me in childhood and imprinted something on my soul. Natalie's work reminds me how art and activism serve each other. How often they must.

I watched the protestors at Standing Rock Reservation from afar as they quickly grew from a handful of water protectors in April 2016 to thousands by the end of the year, plus over a million supporters "checking in" on Facebook in a show of solidarity. The Sioux people were battling the dangerous, encroaching Dakota Access Pipeline (DAPL), a fight few other Americans knew about. That is until a girl named Tokata Iron Eyes, barely a teenager, went on Twitter with friends and unleashed a social media firestorm. Her hashtag #NoDAPL is so widespread it's become an alternate name for the movement. Thousands flocked to Standing Rock; hundreds of thousands more did what they could from their computers. One girl helped start that.

★ ★ ★

I'LL STOP TALKING AT YOU now. I don't have much else to say except, use your voice. Help others. Vote. Thank you for the good work in the world you've done and will do. And I leave you this, from poet, artist, and mother, Layli Long Soldier:

"I do not have the answer to What more does it take? except to say that I know, we all know, it will take more. And toward this, our work continues."

CONCLUSION

---•---

HOPE IS A FORM OF PLANNING.

GLORIA STEINEM

TWELVE MONTHS AFTER the Women's March on Washington, in early December 2017, I flew to Denver to see an exhibit of late-nineteenth-century women artists in Paris, including Mary Cassatt. The show was exclusively female, centering on women who pursued their rebellious and unlikely dreams to the white-hot center of the art world in the decades after Seneca Falls.

I was restless on the plane, rummaging and fidgeting. I was supposed to be reading one book (on deadline), but for some reason (procrastination comes to mind) what I wanted to read instead was a book I'd thrown in my carry-on at the last minute, a history of the Seneca Falls Convention. Research for the very book you are reading now. I caved to impulse early in the flight. There was no one to tell me not to.

I was seated in a row with two young women, clearly friends, who were chatting and checking out pictures on each other's phones. I'd hoped to move back to sit with my friend Tahlia, an artist who's always game for a trip somewhere to look at art, even the sort she's not terribly interested in (if we are lucky, we all have a friend like Tahlia).

But in the end I wasn't able to change seats, so while the young women in my row talked about being bridesmaids, going to parties, and seeing friends, I cracked the book I wasn't supposed to be reading.

Apparently I felt guilty, because I jumped, startled, when just a few pages in, the woman farthest from me suddenly leaned over and spoke. "You have a picture of my great-great-great-great- grandmother in your book," she said, pointing. The book lay open on my

plastic tray to the only page in it with an image of Lucretia Mott. She'd noticed from two seats away.

I counted the greats, looking back and forth between the page before me and the woman in the window seat. It was one of those timeless moments when you think you might hear bells or flapping wings. The word "coincidence" hardly seems meaningful enough for such a close encounter across time.

We talked a bit, but didn't have much to say beyond a polite *how weird!* She wrote her email on the inside cover of my book and we both went back to what we were doing, talking and reading.

It was a remarkable moment of chance, or fate, but in the bustle of travel I soon forgot about her.

When the rubber hit the tarmac, I slapped the book closed, shoved it in my bag, and pushed off the plane, talking to Tahlia over my shoulder. We rushed onto a train, then checked into our hotel. I spent hours at the museum, and afterward we went out to dinner.

It wasn't until I was in bed that night, exhausted, that I remembered the great-great-great-great-granddaughter of Lucretia Mott. I'd never even asked her name. It was like Mott was chiding me from beyond the grave. Groaning, I got up, rooted around in my bag for the book and, finding it, crouched on the hotel carpet and opened the back cover, where Mott's descendent had written her address.

I touched my finger to the page and laughed. Her name was Hope.

ACKNOWL-EDGMENTS

There is profound awe in connecting with women you admire, and in applying the gifts of their work:

Nell Irvin Painter. In addition to graciously providing the foreword to this book, her essential biography, *Sojourner Truth: A Life, A Symbol*, was the primary source for my Truth chapter here, while some two decades ago her book helped spark my own approach to "reading" visual history.

Elaine Weiss. *The Women's Hour: The Great Fight to Win the Vote*, a riveting account of the ratification fight for the Nineteenth Amendment, was published while I was writing this book. A brilliant resource, it is the expansive story of suffrage's most pivotal hour. Read it next.

Sally Roesch Wagner. Her *Sisters in Spirit: Haudenosaunee (Iroquois) Influence on Early American Feminists* was invaluable in revealing a history, context, and culture I knew something of, but not nearly enough.

Linda S. Peavy and Ursula Smith. Though I'd grown up with inklings of the Fort Shaw women's basketball team (we had a "duck hut" near Fort Shaw and my oldest brothers hunted with some descendants of the team), it wasn't until reading *Full Court Quest: The Girls from Fort Shaw Indian School, Basketball Champions of the World* that I discovered how much there was to their incredible story.

Linda Nochlin. Finding her *Women, Art, and Power and Other Essays* in the Metropolitan Museum of Art bookstore changed everything. Later, I saw her give a well-attended lecture on Renoir's *Les Grandes Baigneuses* (*The Large Bathers*) where, after discussing formal elements of the painting, she suddenly jumped as if startled to catch sight of it on the screen. She shook her head and said something like, "I don't want to imply that this is a great painting." Then in glorious detail she listed all the reasons why this supposed masterpiece sucked. I nodded happily along. It was something I'd believed but felt I shouldn't say. Nochlin gave us permission and showed us how.

One hundred fabulous women artists: Em Allen, Tamisha Anthony, Erin Kate Archer, Sarula Bao, Jane Beaird, Kelly Beeman, Alexandra Beguez, Jessica Bogac-Moore, Geneva Bowers, Alexandra Bowman, Julianna Brion, Anna Brones, Jordan Buschur, Lea Carey, Gabriella Cetrulo, Maggie Chiang, Sara Christian, Alexandra Citrin, Rebecca Clarke, Marie Coons, Riza Cruz, Megan Dailey, Umaimah Damakka, Mai Ly Degnan, Ashley Nicole Deleon, Shana Dixon, Ariel Dunitz-Johnson, Cindy Echevarria, Molly Egan, Emily Elliott, Lucy Engelman, Nour I. Flayhan, Tallulah Fontaine, Naomi Franq, Shannon Freshwater, Siobhán Gallagher, Alex Gilbeaux, Sienna Gonzales, Rachel Harrell, Deena Hashem, Maya Ish Shalom, Tessa Jacobs, Angela Johnson, Asia Kang, Orlie Kapitulnik, Jennie Kessinger, Jenice Kim, Sandi Kim, Stephanie Kubo, Nhung Lê, Agnes Lee, Ariel Lee, Audrey Lee, Deborah Lee, Tracy J. Lee, Aura Lewis, Alise Lim, Jianan Liu, Joya Logue, Loris Lora, Ali Mac, Ajuan Mance, Ruso Margishvili, Simone Martin-Newberry, Trisha Mason, Tashana McPherson, Courtney Menard, Chi Michalski, Kara Mitchell, Magdalena Mora, Lauren Moran, Christine

Norrie, Lara Odell, Lydia Ortiz, Haejin Park, Dani Pendergast, Karina Perez, Jess Phoenix, Christa Pierce, Josie Portillo, Krystal Quiles, Monica Ramos, Em Roberts, Cali Sales, Ashley Seil Smith, Divya Seshadri, Whitney Sherman, Jia Sung, Ellen Surrey, Carolyn Suzuki, Lisa Sy, Gica Tam, Ella Trujillo, Libby VanderPloeg, Ana Vee, Kate Wong, Rosalyn Yoon, Vrinda Zaveri, Samya Zitouni, Zsalto. What a thrill to see this bold and beautiful work as it came in. What joy to share it here.

Heartiest thanks to the following dear people:

Bridget Watson Payne. Author, artist, editor, instigator. Three years ago, she sent me an email asking if I knew a writer knowledgeable about U.S. history, "with a funny, accessible, and possibly swear-y writing style?" I am grateful to report that said swear-y writer turned out to be me.

Mirabelle Korn. Editor, whose thoroughness and gentle guidance made this a much better book.

Elsa Dixler. Copy editor. For catching my many extra commas, beaucoup misspellings, and hiccups of logic. Bowing.

Danielle Svetcov. Agent, friend. There's no one whose eye and acumen I trust more and no one more hella entertaining to share stories with.

Mark and Caren Trowbridge. Securers of a speaking gig and place to stay for the Women's March on Washington. Fellow marchers, friends.

Dr. Allegra Alessandri Pfeifer. High school principal, fierce knitter, inspiration. Artisan of the exemplary pussy hat I donned that day.

Carol Edgarian. Mentor and great pal, along with the many good peeps at *Narrative* magazine, especially Tom Jenks, Jane Lancellotti, and Katie Dickson.

The Writers Grotto in San Francisco. Spectacular community, with special thanks to: Larry Rosen, incomparably amusing foil and inimitable podcaster. Julie Lythcott-Haims, who responded to anxious emails and made time to talk even when deep in her own projects. Anisse Gross, for weekend work marathons, and who alongside Xandra Castleton and Julia Scheeres has offered an essential circle of mutual support. And Vanessa Hua, beloved work wife who responds to despairing messages with kind but firm bucking up, whose art and energy always inspires. May her name be blessed.

Ginny Van Dine. Ace research assistant, and co-host of the *Art History Babes* podcast (highly recommended).

Jami Attenberg. Novelist and Twitter do-gooder. Her light-a-fire-under-your-ass #1000wordsofsummer helped me break open an early draft of this book.

Tahlia Priete, for our artful adventures, with more I hope to come; Rafferty Atha Jackson and Erica Teasley Linnick, for that Memphis weekend where we did not find Ida B. Wells where I'd hoped to, but did find much moving history (and great barbecue).

Michelle Dodd, Marie-Claire Gelbard, Jessica Kanat, Stacey Hubbard, Annette Hughes-White, Chaylee Priete, Tahlia Priete, Jennifer March Soloway, Jillian Steadman, Durelle

Schacter, and Sharon Welter—women upon whom my sanity, and gladness, relies.

Dear sisters: Padeen Quinn and Diane Regan-Sandbak. Good brothers: Brendhan, Patrick, Tom, John, Chris, and Bill. Beautiful mother, Polly. Bigger-than-life dad, Jake.

Rick and Lukas and Zuzu: my heart. You three most especially. Love and thank you.

SELECT BIBLIOGRAPHY

Baker, Jean H. *Sisters: The Lives of America's Suffragists.* New York: Hill and Wang, 2005.

Beard, Mary. *Women & Power: A Manifesto.* New York: Norton, 2017.

Bernard, Michelle. "Despite the Tremendous Risk, African American Women Marched for Suffrage, Too." *Washington Post,* March 3, 2013.

Bess, Gaby. "Alternatives to Alternatives: The Black Grrrls Riot Ignored." *Broadly,* August 3, 2015.

Boissoneault, Lorraine. "The Suffragist Statue Trapped in a Broom Closet for 75 Years." *Smithsonian.com.* May 12, 2017.

Brinlee, Morgan. "Naomi Wadler Is March for Our Lives' Youngest Speaker & Twitter Wants Her for President." *Bustle,* March 24, 2018.

Brooke, James. "3 Suffragists (in Marble) to Move Up in the Capitol." *The New York Times,* September 26, 1996.

Broude, Norma. "Mary Cassatt: Modern Woman or the Cult of True Womanhood?" *Woman's Art Journal* 21, no. 2 (Fall 2000/Winter 2001): 36-43.

Chave, Anna C. "The Guerrilla Girls' Reckoning." *Art Journal* 70, no. 2 (Summer 2011): 102–11.

Clift, Eleanor. *Votes for Women: Founding Sisters and the Nineteenth Amendment.* Hoboken, NJ: John Wiley & Sons, 2003.

Coontz, Stephanie. *A Strange Stirring: The Feminine Mystique and American Women at the Dawn of the 1960s.* New York: Basic Books, 2011.

Dennison, Mariea Caudill. "Babies for Suffrage: The Exhibition of Painting and Sculpture by Women Artists for the Benefit of the Woman Suffrage Campaign." *Woman's Art Journal* 20, no. 2 (Autumn 2003/Winter 2004): 24-30.

Dickerson, Caitlin. "Ida B. Wells." Overlooked, *The New York Times,* March 8, 2018.

D'Souza, Aruna and Michael Lobel, Kenneth E. Silver, Elizabeth C. Baker. "Remembering Linda Nochlin." *Art in America,* January 1, 2018.

Dudden, Faye E. *Fighting Chance: The Struggle Over Woman Suffrage and Black Suffrage in Reconstruction America.* New York: Oxford University Press, 2011.

Eller, Claudia. "Emma González Opens Up About How Her Life Has Changed Since Parkland Tragedy." *Variety,* October 9, 2018.

Faxon, Alicia. "Painter and Patron: Collaboration of Mary Cassatt and Louisine Havemeyer." *Woman's Art Journal* 3 (Fall 1982/ Winter 1983): 15–20.

Flexner, Eleanor and Ellen Fitzpatrick. *Century of Struggle: The Women's Rights Movement in the United States.* Enlarged Edition. Cambridge, MA: The Belknap Press of Harvard University Press, 1996.

Frere-Jones, Sasha. "Hanna and Her Sisters." *The New Yorker,* November 19, 2012.

Friedan, Betty. *The Feminine Mystique.* New York: Norton, 1963.

Heilbrun, Carolyn G. *Writing a Woman's Life.* New York: Norton, 1988.

Hess, Thomas B. and Elizabeth C. Baker, eds. *Art and Sexual Politics.* New York: Macmillan, 1973.

Hix, Lisa. "War on Women, Waged in Postcards: Memes from the Suffragist Era." *Collectors Weekly,* November 1, 2012.

Hunter, Marjorie. "Remembering Rankin." *The New York Times,* April 27, 1985.

"Inspiring Women's Rights: Haudenosaunee Life Stimulates Historical Movement." Oneida Indian Nation, www.oneidaindiannation.com/inspiring-womens-rights-haudenosaunee-life-stimulates-historical-movement/.

"Kim Gordon Chats With Kathleen Hanna: Uncut Version!" *Bust*, October/November 2013.

Kolber, Ramsay. "An Exhibition About Revolution That Keeps Faith with Ringgold." *Hyperallergic*, September 15, 2017.

Lee, Ellen. "Patsy Takemoto Mink's Trailblazing Testimony Against a Supreme Court Nominee." *The Atlantic*, September 16, 2018.

Levin, Sam. "At Standing Rock, Women Lead the Fight in Face of Mace, Arrests and Strip Searches." *The Guardian*, November 4, 2016.

Long Soldier, Layli. "Women and Standing Rock: Introduction." *Orion Magazine* 36, no. 4 (2017).

Lorde, Audre. *Your Silence Will Not Protect You.* London: Silver Press, 2017.

Mankiller, Wilma. *Mankiller: A Chief and Her People.* New York: St. Martin's Press, 1999.

Marcus, Sara. *Girls to the Front: The True Story of the Riot Grrrl Revolution.* New York: Harper Perennial, 2010.

Mathews, Nancy Mowll. *Mary Cassatt: A Life.* New Haven: Yale University Press, 1994.

McMillen, Sally G. *Seneca Falls and the Origins of the Women's Rights Movement.* New York: Oxford University Press, 2008.

Murphy, Mary. "When Jeannette Said 'No,' Montana Women's Response to World War I." *Montana: The Magazine of Western History*, Spring 2015.

Murphy, Mekado. "The Guerrilla Girls, After 3 Decades, Still Rattling Art World Cages." *The New York Times*, August 5, 2015.

Nirappil, Fenit. "The Story Behind 11-Year-Old Naomi Wadler and Her March for Our Lives Speech." *The Washington Post*, March 25, 2018.

Nochlin, Linda. *Women, Art, and Power and Other Essays.* New York: Harper & Row, 1988.

Painter, Nell Irvin. *Sojourner Truth: A Life, a Symbol.* New York: Norton, 1996.

Peavy, Linda and Ursula Smith. *Full-Court Quest: The Girls from Fort Shaw Indian School Basketball Champions of the World.* Norman: University of Oklahoma Press, 2008.

Phelps, Timothy M. "I Broke the Anita Hill Story. Here's What We Need to Learn From Her Treatment." Op-ed, *Los Angeles Times*, September 18, 2018.

Pogrebin, Abigail. "How Do You Spell Ms." *New York* magazine, October 30, 2011.

Prince, Tracy J. and Zadie Schaffer. *Notable Women of Portland.* Charleston, South Carolina: Arcadia Publishing, 2017.

Raizada, Kristen. "An Interview With the Guerrilla Girls, Dyke Action Machine (DAM!), and the Toxic Titties." *NWSA Journal*, Spring 2007.

Reilly, Maura, ed. *The Linda Nochlin Reader.* New York: Thames & Hudson, 2015.

Rich, Adrienne. *Culture, Politics, and the Art of Poetry: Essential Essays.* New York: Norton, 2018.

Roberts, Rebecca Boggs. *Suffragists in Washington, D.C.: The 1913 Parade and the Fight for the Vote.* Charleston, SC: The History Press, 2017.

Ryzik, Melena. "A Feminist Riot That Still Inspires." *The New York Times*, June 3, 2011.

Sharp, Sarah Rose. "Do Women Rock? The Met Overlooks Women's Contribution to Rock and Roll." *Hyperallergic*, November 28, 2018.

Shear, Michael D. "Students Lead Huge Rallies for Gun Control Across the U.S." *The New York Times*, March 24, 2018.

Switzer, Kathrine. *Marathon Woman: Running the Race to Revolutionize Women's Sports*. New York: Carroll & Graff, 2007.

Steinem, Gloria. *My Life on the Road*. New York: Random House, 2015.

Stone, Ann E.W. "Moving the Women Into the Light." National Women's History Museum, May 23, 2017.

Tognotti, Chris. "Transcript of Emma González's March for Our Lives Speech Will Absolutely Crush You." *Bustle*, May 24, 2018.

Verhovek, Sam Howe. "The Name's the Most and Least of Her." *The New York Times*, November 4, 1993.

Wagner, Sally Roesch. *Sisters in Spirit: Haudenosaunee (Iroquois) Influence on Early American Feminists*. Summertown, TN: Native Voices, 2001.

Wagner, Sally Roesch. "How Native American Women Inspired the Feminist Movement." *BUST* magazine, October/November, 2015.

Walsh, Edward. "Carol Braun's Rocky Road to History." *The Washington Post*, April 28, 1992.

Weinraub, Judith. "Mankiller." *The Washington Post*, December 10, 1993.

Weiss, Elaine. *The Woman's Hour: The Great Fight to Win the Vote*. New York: Viking, 2018.

Wells, Ida B. *The Light of Truth: Writings of an Anti-Lynching Crusader*. Edited by Mia Bay and Henry Louis Gates. New York: Penguin, 2014.

Winton, Ben. "The Occupation of Alcatraz." *The Native Press*, May 1, 2010.

Wilson, Joan Hoff. "Jeannette Rankin and American Foreign Policy: The Origins of Her Pacifism." *Montana: The Magazine of Western History*, Winter 1980.

Withers, Josephine. "The Guerrilla Girls." *Feminist Studies* 14, no. 2 (Summer 1988): 285.

"Women and Power." *The Cut*, October 14, 2018.

CREDITS

p. 102
Em Allen is a Minneapolis-based illustrator. *www.allenem.com*

p. 134
Tamisha Anthony is the artist and illustrator behind the paper goods and products line Xo Puffed Sleeves, and lives in New York City. *@tamisha.anthony*

p. 208
Erin Kate Archer is an artist, children's book illustrator, and Skillshare teacher based in Brooklyn. *@ekatearcher*

pp. 52–53
Sarula Bao is a Chinese American illustrator and graphic novelist based in Brooklyn. *@bao__haus*

p. 90
Jane Beaird is a Brooklyn-based illustrator and fine artist who works under the name Quiet Creature. *@quietcreature*

p. 32
Kelly Beeman is an artist and fashion illustrator residing in Brooklyn. *www.kellybeeman.com*

p. 128
Alexandra Beguez is a New Jersey–based illustrator and cartoonist, whose clients have included *Buzzfeed*, *The Nib*, and BOOM Studios. *@bisforbeguez*

p. 22
Jessica Bogac-Moore is an illustrator who creates picture books, fine art, and comics, and currently lives in Oakland. *jbogacmoore.wixsite.com/mysite*

p. 65
Geneva Bowers is a self-taught illustrator based in Western North Carolina. *@gdbee*

pp. 186–187
Alexandra Bowman is a current student at Georgetown University, where she is double majoring in English and History, and minoring in Studio Art. *@alexandrabowmanart*

pp. 70–71
Julianna Brion is a Baltimore-based illustrator whose clients include *The New York Times*, *The New Yorker*, Penguin Books, and more. *@juliannabrion*

p. 165
Anna Brones is an artist and food writer, and the founder and publisher of *Comestible*. *@annabrones*

p. 126
Jordan Buschur is an artist, educator, and curator living in Toledo, Ohio. *jordanbuschur.com*

p. 172
Lea Carey is a New York City–based artist with a background in textiles and graphic design. *@leancarey*

p. 72
Gabriella Cetrulo is a New York–based artist and illustrator whose clients include *Teen Vogue*, *BUST* magazine, and H&M. *@gabriellacetrulo*

pp. 168–169
Maggie Chiang is a Taiwanese American artist based in Los Angeles, whose clients include *The New York Times*, *The New Yorker*, and *The Washington Post*. *@mcmintea*

p. 162
Sara Christian is a designer and illustrator residing in Oakland. *www.sarachristian.info*

p. 92
Alexandra Citrin is a New York City–based illustrator, art director, and visiting professor of illustration and design-based research at Pratt Institute. *@alexcitrin*

p. 116
Rebecca Clarke is an illustrator who has worked with Laurence King Publishing, *The New York Times*, and *The New Yorker*, among others; she lives in Key West, Florida. *@rebeccaclarke*

p. 76
Marie Coons is a Brooklyn–based illustrator and designer, whose clients have included HBO, PBS, and Nikon World. *@mcswiss*

p. 152
Riza Cruz is an illustrator, designer, and paper crafter living in the San Francisco Bay Area. *@tinypaperlab*

p. 202
Megan Dailey is an illustrator living in Santa Fe, New Mexico, whose work has been featured by Google, Clif Bar, Feminist Majority Foundation, and others. *@megandaileydraws*

p. 94
Umaimah Damakka is an animation student at Savannah College of Art and Design, where her focus is on character design and illustration. *@coloured_braids*

p. 156
Mai Ly Degnan is an illustrator, pattern designer, card maker, and illustration professor living in Baltimore. *@mailydegnan*

pp. 84–85
Ashley Nicole Deleon is an illustrator, comic artist, and bookbinder living in Brooklyn. *@ashnicdel*

p. 82
Shana Dixon is an animator and illustrator living in New Jersey. *@shanaabanaa*

p. 104
Ariel Dunitz-Johnson is an illustrator specializing in portraiture living in San Francisco. *@arieldraws*

p. 30
Cindy Echevarria is an illustrator living in Miami. *@cinderblkk*

p. 142
Molly Egan is a Philadelphia-based illustrator whose work has been featured in *Bravery Magazine*, *Bust magazine*, and *Bitch Media*, among others. *@mollytheillustrator*

p. 88
Emily Elliott is a painter and illustrator based in Boise. *www.emily-elliott.com*

p. 80
Lucy Engelman is a Pittsburgh-based illustrator who has collaborated with chefs and farmers, created imagery for apparel and home goods, and made custom wallpapers. *@lucyengelman*

p. 190
Nour I. Flayhan is a Lebanese American illustrator currently based in London. *@nouriflayhan*

p. 146
Tallulah Fontaine is a Canadian illustrator and artist currently living in Los Angeles and Montreal.
@tallulahfontaine

pp. 194–195
Naomi Franq is a Florida-based illustrator and comic book artist, whose clients have included BOOM!, Marvel, and Image.
@naomifranq

p. 47
Shannon Freshwater is a Los Angeles–based illustrator, professor in the art department at California State University Northridge, and illustration faculty at The Art Center.
www.shannonfreshwater.com

p. 132
Siobhán Gallagher is a Canadian illustrator, designer, and author of the book *In a Daze Work*, currently living in New York City.
@siogallagher

p. 59
Alex Gilbeaux is an illustrator and animator who has worked with *Refinery29*, Comedy Central, TED Talk, and others.
@alex.gilbeaux

p. 158
Sienna Gonzales is a writer and visual artist based in Los Angeles.
@somewhere_in_june

p. 110
Rachel Harrell is a visual designer and illustrator based in San Francisco.
*@rachelharrell_*

p. 111
Deena Hashem is an artist based in Oakland.
deenahashem.com

pp. 120–121
Maya Ish Shalom is an illustrator originally from Tel Aviv, now residing in Brooklyn.
@maya_ishshalom

p. 61
Tess K. Jacobs is an artist, writer, and folklorist based in Santa Barbara, California.

p. 144
Angela Johnson is an artist whose work is inspired by nature, and lives in South Kona, Hawaii.
www.angelainthesea.com

p. 4
Asia Kang is a Bay Area illustrator who specializes in visual design and comics.
@asiakang

p. 15
Orlie Kapitulnik is an illustrator and production artist, and a printmaking instructor at 3Fish Studios; she lives in San Francisco.
@orliegrams

p. 74
Jennie Kessinger is a practicing lawyer and artist living in San Francisco.
@jennie_kessinger

p. 78
Jenice Kim is an illustrator and designer who was raised in Korea and Canada, and now lives in New York.
@jenicekimm

p. 170
Sandi Kim is an illustrator and graphic artist who currently creates designs for phone cases, greeting cards, apparel, gifts, and packaging.
@sandiillustrator

p. 155
Stephanie Kubo is an illustrator based in Brooklyn whose clients have included Google Play, *The Boston Globe*, and *Bitch* magazine.
@stephaniekubo

p. 62
Nhung Lê is a Vietnamese illustrator living in Brooklyn.
@chicnawdie

p. 44
Agnes Lee is an illustrator and occasional art director living in Brooklyn.
@ahjleee

p. 77
Ariel Lee is an artist and illustrator based in Southern California whose clients have included *The New York Times*, Teach For America, and *The Wall Street Journal*.
*@lee_ariel_*

p. 201
Audrey Lee has worked in various motion design studios as a designer, illustrator, and art director, and lives in Los Angeles, California.
@audjree

p. 68
Deborah Lee is a Korean illustrator now living in San Francisco.
@jdebbiel

pp. 106–107
Tracy J. Lee is an artist and a senior designer at the clothing company Hatch.
@tracyjleeart

p. 125
Aura Lewis is a New York City-based illustrator and author of two books, *Gloria's Voice* and *The Illustrated Feminist*.
@auralewis

p. 88
Alise Lim is an illustrator based in Brooklyn, who holds a BFA in illustration from Ringling College of Art and Design.
@alice.lim

p. 96
Jianan Liu is an illustrator originally from Beijing, now residing in Baltimore.
@jiananliuillustration

p. 66
Joya Logue is a Bengali American watercolor artist currently living in the Midwest, whose work has been featured in *Elle Home Décor India*, *Elle Japan*, *Vogue Japan*, and more.
@rajovilla

pp. 138–139
Loris Lora is a Los Angeles–based illustrator and designer who has worked in editorial publishing, book publishing, children's toy design, and surface design.
@loris_lora

p. 136
Ali Mac is a freelance illustrator and the founder of Love Lore, a boutique specializing in bespoke wedding and event stationery.
@alimacdoodle

p. 184
Ajuan Mance is a visual artist, English professor at Mills College, and author of *Inventing Black Women* and *Before Harlem*; she is based in Oakland.
http://8-rock.com/

pp. 204–205
Ruso Margishvili is a New York City–based architect and illustrator.
@rusomarg

p. 60
Simone Martin-Newberry is a Chicago-based graphic designer and illustrator.
@unclesweaters

p. 148
Trisha Mason is an artist based in Indianapolis, Indiana.
@trishabmason

p. 42
Tashana McPherson is a Jamaican illustrator and fashion illustrator currently living in Brooklyn.
@tashillustration

p. 114
Courtney Menard is a Brooklyn-based illustrator, printmaker, and co-curator for the 2019 Comic Arts Brooklyn festival.
@asmallmenard

p. 64
Chi Michalski is an illustrator and occasional art director living in Seattle.
@chichiland

p. 188
Kara Mitchell is an illustrator living in Oklahoma City, Oklahoma, whose main focus is children's book illustration and illustrated graphics.
@kara_m_mitchell

p. 131
Magdalena Mora is an illustrator and graphic designer with a special interest in children's books and visual storytelling; she lives in Minneapolis.
@magdalena.i.mora

p. 108
Lauren Moran is an illustrator and graphic tee designer living in Manhattan, New York.
@laurenmoran

pp. 182–183
Christine Norrie is a New York City-based artist and author of graphic novels, including *Cheat*, *Hopeless Savages*, and *Breaking Up*.
@christinenorrie

p. 38
Lara Odell is an artist living in Southern California, whose work has appeared in *The New York Times*, *The Washington Post*, and *Air France Magazine*, among others.
@laraodell

p. 8
Lydia Ortiz is an art director, designer, and illustrator currently based in the San Francisco Bay Area.
www.lydiaortiz.com/

p. 173
Haejin Park is a Korean illustrator and graphic designer currently residing in Brooklyn, and has worked with publications including *The New York Times*, *WeTransfer*, and *BuzzFeed*.
@haejinduck

p. 40
Dani Pendergast is a freelance illustrator living in Syracuse, New York, and has held workshops and events at The Ark, Syracuse University, and Urban Outfitters, among other places.
@dcpender

p. 34
Karina Perez is a Mexican American illustrator and designer based in Savannah, Georgia.
@kinnycupsart

p. 198
Jess Phoenix is a Seattle-based illustrator, designer, and pattern-creator, whose work has been featured on stationery, book covers, embroidery, and more.
@jessraephoenix

p. 118
Christa Pierce is an illustrator and the author of *Did You Know That I Love You?*; she lives in Portland, Oregon.
@christapierce_papergoods

p. 116
Josie Portillo is an illustrator living in Los Angeles, whose clients include American Express, *The New York Times*, and *The Washington Post*.
@josie_portillo

p. 26
Krystal Quiles is a Brooklyn-based illustrator and graduate of the Pratt Institute.
@krystalquiles

p. 197
Monica Ramos is an illustrator born and raised in the Philippines, now living in Brooklyn.
@moniiqwa

p. 49
Em Roberts is a freelance illustrator, hand letterer, and designer, living in Baltimore.
@wickermaiden

p. 19
Cali Sales is an illustrator living in Austin, Texas, whose work has appeared in *The New York Times*, *She Shreds Magazine*, and others.
http://www.calisales.com

p. 56
Ashley Seil Smith is an illustrator, painter, and printmaker based in New York City.
@seilsmith

p. 150
Divya Seshadri is an artist who has been featured in *Shots Magazine* and *Drum Mag*, and has served on juries including Addy's and The One Club Bootcamp.
@divyaseshadri

p. 18
Whitney Sherman is an illustrator, educator, and entrepreneur, and is currently the director of the MFA in Illustration Practice at Maryland Institute College of Art.
www.whitneysherman.com

p. 100
Jia Sung is an art director at *Guernica* and teaching artist in residence at the Hudson River Museum; she lives in Brooklyn.
@jiazilla

p. 98
Ellen Surrey is an illustrator living in Los Angeles, who works in collaboration with the illustration collective Clover Scouts.
@yesurrey

p. 178
Carolyn Suzuki is an illustrator and the owner of a greeting card business based in Los Angeles, California.
@carolynsuzuki

p. 123
Lisa Sy is a multi-disciplinary software and product designer, illustrator, and artist living in Los Angeles.
@lisasyart

p. 54
Gica Tam is a designer and illustrator based in New York City.
@gicatam

pp. 176–177
Ella Trujillo is an illustrator, artist, and designer based in Taos, New Mexico, whose clients include *The New York Times*, *The Atlantic*, and *Pitchfork*.
@ella_trujillo

jacket, p. 12
Libby VanderPloeg is an illustrator and designer whose clients have included *The Wall Street Journal*, *The New York Times*, and *The Washington Post*; she lives in Brooklyn.
@libbyvanderploeg

p. 192
Ana Vee Valdez is a San Francisco–based illustrator and comic artist, and the founder of the Girls Who Eat Zine project.
@badddcat

p. 210
Kate Wong is an illustrator living in Santa Clara, California, whose clients include *Darling Magazine*, *Orange Coast Magazine*, and Workman Publishing.
@striped_cat_studio

p. 20
Rosalyn Yoon is a Korean American illustrator living in Pittsburgh, Pennsylvania.
@rosalynyoon

p. 143
Vrinda Zaveri is a San Francisco-based artist working at Roguemark Studios.
www.vrindazaveri.com

p. 112
Samya Zitouni is an animation student at Laguna College of Art and Design, living in Aliso Viejo, California.
@smyazitouni

p. 160
Zsalto is an artist, illustrator, and molecular biologist living in California.
@zsalto

INDEX